the

DREAMBOOK

What would you attempt to do

IF YOU KNEW IT WAS

IMPOSSIBLE
to fail?

THE DREAM BOOK

SPECIAL THANKS

It is impossible for any person to deserve full credit for any work accomplished, as our lives in reality, are 'a collection' of contributors and influencers.

Firstly, I would like to thank the precious Holy Spirit for His constant guidance in my life and in this project. You truly are 'my Wonderful Counsellor' and you are 'the True Author'. Without your presence in my life, life would be meaningless…

My beloved wite Lydia, you are my 'shining light', I love and appreciate you with all my heart. Thank you for all your input on this project and allowing me the time needed to fulfill this dream. You are a constant well of living water.

A special thanks to Pastor Rodney and Valda Sneddon, my in laws, you stood with me in the transition. When I came home you put 'the best robe' (righteousness) around me, you put 'a ring' (authority) on my finger, and 'shoes' (son's wear shoes) on my feet, thank you…

To all who have been a constant encouragement in my life, thank you. My deepest desire is for all your desires to be fulfilled.

THE DREAMBOOK
Introduction

"A good man out of the good treasure of the heart bringeth forth good things..."
Matthew 12:35

This dreambook has been designed to show you practically how to bring forth your dreams and desires into the earth from within your heart.

For the Wright brothers it was flight that inspired the invention of the first airplane.

It was his dream of light that possessed Thomas Edison to invent the light bulb.

It was the first automobile that burned in Henry Fords heart. His dream is the reason we are travelling by car on our roads today.

Where there is no vision there is no creation. Think about this: before a building is built the developer has a mental picture of what he wants to build, he transfers his ideas over to an architect to translate onto paper. From there it goes to a graphic designer who creates an artists impression of the building, which is printed and placed on a billboard long before the foundation has even been layed.

All creation starts with a vision and dream in the unseen realm.

"Where there is no vision of your destiny people perish."
Proverbs 29:18.

Where there is no clear picture of your destiny people perish. Vision is having a strong mental image or a clear picture of your destiny.

Hellen Keller was asked, "What would be worse than being born blind?" To which she replied, "to have sight with no vision."

Vision is the ability to see, not with the physical eye but with the inner eye of faith.

For true visionaries, the imagininary world is more real to them than the physical three dimensional. In fact, a visionary's vision is his reality. When Disney world had just opened and had one ride, Walt Disney was sitting on a bench on the grounds, seeming to just stare into space. One of his employees who maintained the gardens came past him and said, "How are you sir?"
Without looking at the man, he said, "Fine," and kept on staring. So the man said, "Mr Disney, what are you doing?"
"I'm looking at my mountain," he answered. "I see the mountain right there." Walt had told his architects about this mountain. As he talked, they wrote down what he said, and then they drew up the plans. Walt died before Space Mountain was ever built, so he never saw it constructed. When Space Mountain was dedicated, the governor and mayor were present, along with Walt's widow. One of the young men stood up to introduce her, and said, "it's a pity that Mr. Walt Disney is not here today to see this mountain, but we're glad his wife is here."

Mrs Disney walked up to the podium, looked at the crowd and said, in effect, "I must correct this young man. Walt already saw the mountain. It's you who are just now seeing it."

Vision is not sight, it's insight. Vision is having a clear picture of conditions that does not currently exist in the natural realm. It's having a strong mental image or picture of your destiny. Now it's your turn to bring forth your dreams! It's your turn to bring forth the potential that God has placed in you to impact your generation.

God told Abraham, "lift up now your eyes and look from the place where thou art northward, and southward, and eastward and westward: For all the land that thou seest, to thee will I give it, and to thy seed forever."

What did God tell Abraham? Until you see it you are not entitled to get it! What you see will become your boundry. Whatever you can see, he is commited to delivering it. What you see today is what you will experience tomorrow. It's a law of the spirit!

We liken 'the heart or spirit' of a man to a 'painter's canvas'. What we dream and envision is 'the paint' and if we take the 'brush of faith' and begin to paint our 'dreams and visions' given by God on the canvas of our heart, they will become a reality.

"Keep your heart with all vigilance, and above all that you guard, for out of it flow the springs of life."
Proverbs 4 :23

God had a dream for the children of Israel. He told Moses to send men from every tribe (Leaders) to search the land, "which I give unto the children of Israel." Numbers 13:1 - 2.

Caleb was one of the men sent and he saw the land with the eyes of faith. "And Caleb stilled the people before Moses, and said, 'Let us go up at once and posses it for we are well able to overcome it." Numbers 13: 30.

Caleb saw what God had promised. He saw the promise. What do you see? The others couldn't see themselves in the land that God had promised them.

But the men that went up with him said, "We be not able to go up against the people for they are stronger than we. And they brought up an evil report of the land which they had searched unto the children of Israel saying, 'the land, through which we have gone to search it, is a land that eateth up the inhabitants thereof; and all the people that saw in it are men of great stature. And there we saw the giants: the sons of Anak, which come of the giants, and we were in our own sight grasshoppers, and so we were in their sight.'"
Numbers 13:31-33.

They were looking at themselves, and their own abilities, instead of focusing on the promise of God. While Joshua and Caleb were focused on what God had promised.

"Behold I send an angel before thee to keep thee in the way and to bring thee into the place which I have prepared." *Exodus 23:20-23*

Only Joshua and Caleb saw what God had promised. The other 2 to 3 million people with the 10 leaders that came back with the bad report all died in the wilderness never seeing and receiving what God had promised them!

What do you see today, the promise or the problem? You must develop the "eye of faith" in order for you to enter into what God has promised for you.

THE CREATION STORY

GOD IS A DREAMER

 He had 'a dream' in His *heart*,
a beautiful home for a

father and his family.

This was the reason for creation. He imagined and envisioned a place so beautiful, so rich in all kinds of treasures, deposits of silver and gold, uncounted varieties of metals, precious stones, and resources that would respond to the touch of His children. He covered the face of the earth with mountains, valleys and ravines. He clothed the countryside with a garment of green intermingled with beautiful coloured flowers. The mountainsides He covered with giant forests, whose trees are filled with singing birds and droning insects. In His heart were the fish of the sea and animals of every kind.
In His heart was a dream.

INCUBATING
Def. To maintain (something, such as an embryo or a chemically active system)
under conditions favorable for development, or reaction.
To cause or aid the development of an idea.

In the beginning God (Elohim) created [by forming from nothing] the heavens and the the face of the deep [primeval ocean that covered the unformed earth]. The Spirit of

By faith we understand that the universe was formed at God's command, so

ENVISIONING
Def. Conceiving or imagining.
Especially clear and detailed imagining and picturing something that is not yet seen.
A mental picture of something that does not currently exist naturally.

BROODING
Def. To sit over, cover, to cherish as a hen broods ovr her chicks

earth. The earth was *formless* and *void* or a waste and emptiness, and **darkness** was upon God was moving (*hovering, brooding*) over the face of the waters. *Genesis 1:1-2 (Amp)*

that what is seen was not made out of what was visible. *Hebrews 11:3 (NIV)*

THE SPIRIT OF GOD

in
GENESIS 1:3-27

the Bible says:

And God said, **"Let there be light,"** and there was light. 4 God saw that the light was good, and He separated the light from the darkness. 5 God called the light "day," and the darkness He called "night." And there was evening, and there was morning—the first day.

And God said.
And God said..
And God said...

GOD SAID:

And God said...
Then God said, "Let us make mankind in our image..."

He envisioned, incubated and imagined what He wanted. Then He released it with words full of faith and power to change the earth. God pulled all that He needed out of heaven's resources.

"LET THERE BE LIGHT"

and then in
GENESIS 1:31

the Bible says:

GOD SAW

God saw all that he had made, and it was very good. And there was evening, and there was morning—the sixth day.

THIS IS HOW GOD CREATED WHAT HE SAW:

GOD ENVISIONED

GOD FILLED HIS HEART WITH A DREAM

GOD BELIEVED IT IN HIS HEART

GOD SAID

GOD SAW IT

CONSIDER THESE QUESTIONS

WHO IS DOING THE CREATING?

GOD, WHO IS A SPIRIT

"God is a spirit, and his worshipers must worship him in spirit and in truth."

John 4:24

WHERE DID GOD GET THE SEEDS FROM

To plant the garden?

The garden of Eden was
PLANTED OUT OF HEAVEN
IF YOU SAW THE GARDEN OF EDEN YOU WOULD SEE HEAVEN.

"And I have put My words in your mouth; I have covered you with the shadow of My hand, That **I may plant the heavens**, Lay the foundations of the earth, And say to Zion, 'You are My people.'"

Isaiah 51:16 (NKJV)

Also see: *Revelation 22:1–2 Revelation 21:2, 18-21*

WHERE DID GOD GET THE LIGHT FROM?

From the inside out.
The light came from an invisible kingdom within God.

*"The LORD merely spoke, and the heavens were created.
He breathed the word, and all the stars were born."*

Psalm 33:6 (NLT)

HE IS A
STAR BREATHER

God created the universe at the speed of light, at 299,279 kilometers per second.

The same kingdom is inside you.
You are made just like Him.
You are to live from the inside out using the same process.

"Nor will they say, 'See here!' or 'See there!' For indeed, the kingdom of God is within you." Luke 17:21 (NKJV)

God operated between two realms: the spirit and the physical. God was not moved by what He saw in the physical. The world was a blank canvas… an empty waste. God knew that regardless of what He saw in the natural, He could change it by pulling all that He needed from the realm of the spirit.

If you look at Adam before the fall, he could see these two realms and he walked between them. He saw all the provision that was laid up, and if he needed anything he just called for it. Adam imitated his father. Adam knew who he was, and he knew what was available to him. That is what gave him the authority and ability to name all the animals, and to care for the garden. Nothing was missing, nothing lacking, and nothing broken. There were no universities in the garden. Adam never learnt, he discerned. Not only did Adam name over 1 million species of animals on the earth but he also had the capacity to remember each one. He truly reflected God's nature!

When Adam sinned he lost this spiritual eyesight and the Bible says, "his (natural) eyes were opened!" He lost his access to all the provisions in the Kingdom of God and the earth became his boundary. But, thank God that He made a way for us.

THERE IS

OPERATE BETWEEN TWO REALMS

Luke 4:18
"The Spirit of the Lord is upon me because he hath anointed me to preach the gospel to the poor; He hath sent me to heal the brokenhearted, to preach deliverance to the captives, and recovering of sight to the blind, to set at liberty them that are bruised."

Here Jesus is not only referring to blind eyes; He is talking about spiritual blindness.
The blindness of the mind.
He's talking about the ability (or inability) to see and perceive spiritual things. God knew that you and I can only go as far as we can see and as long as we see this physical three-dimensional world as our boundary, we cannot go very far. The enemy's plan is to keep us in spiritual blindness toward the workings of the Spirit. This way he keeps us within the boundaries of this physical three-dimensional realm. He wants to stop us from seeing and operating in the invisible, more powerful realm of the Spirit.
Everything physical is controlled by the more powerful realm of the Spirit.

A scriptural example where the importance of seeing between both realms is highlighted can be found in the story of Gehazi in 2 Kings 6:4-8.

The king of Syria had sent a great army to surround the city of Dothan with the sole purpose to kill the prophet, Elisha. Gehazi, Elisha's servant, was fearful because he only saw the situation with his natural eyes. Elisha, on the other hand, saw into the spiritual realm with his spiritual eyes.

It was with this sight that he answered Gehazi, "Do not fear, for those who are with us are more than those who are with them." Elisha prayed, "Lord, I pray, open his eyes that he may see."
The Lord opened the eyes of Gehazi and behold, the mountain was full of horses and chariots of fire surrounded Elisha!
The Lord's will is that your spiritual eyes would open as Gehazi's did. It wasn't just for the prophet: it was for the servant too!
Just because you have never seen into the unseen realm doesn't mean it isn't right here under your nose. It was right there the whole time in front of Gehazi. As he peered out of the window, all he could see was the temporal realm — Syria's chariots and army — and it caused him fear.
Elisha, however, remained calm, more moved by what was going on in the spiritual realm than what was going on in the natural since everything comes out of the spiritual realm in the first place!

When God said, "Let there be light," light came out of the invisible. That same realm still exists and is in operation today! God wants us to tap into it! That's why it says in Matthew 4:17, "The kingdom of heaven is at hand."

WHAT IS RESERVED FOR YOU?

There is an invisible kingdom within you that has everything you will ever desire or need according to life and godliness.

God's word says that He has put aside an inheritance "that can never perish, spoil or fade. This inheritance is kept in heaven for you."
1 Peter 1:4-5 (NIV)

The creation story shows us that we have access to the Kingdom where our Father has **reserved** an inheritance for us.

So what is reserved for us in this Kingdom?
Friends, the list is boundless. We're talking about abundant preplanned provision.

Protection
is reserved for you.
God's promises
are reserved for you.
Solutions to every problem
are reserved for you.
Body parts
are reserved for you.
Opportunities
are reserved for you.
Houses, cars and any supplies
are reserved for you.
(For reference, read 2 Peter 1:3, Ephesians 1:3-4, 2:10 Psalm 139:16)

IT'S ALL THERE.

WHAT'S UP THERE?

Everything you will ever need.

ALL THE THINGS GOD HAS FOR US HAVE ALREADY BEEN PREPARED AND PUT AWAY FOR US.

He has pre-arranged every car you will drive, every house you will live in, every book you will ever write or business idea you will conceive.

He has even laid up spare body parts for those that need them.

AND HE DID ALL THIS BEFORE THE FOUNDATIONS OF THE WORLD.

OPEN THE EYES OF YOUR UNDERSTANDING BY SAYING THIS CONFESSION DAILY

I keep asking that the God of our Lord Jesus Christ, the glorious Father, may give you the Spirit of wisdom and revelation, so that you may know Him better. I pray that the eyes of your heart may be enlightened in order that you may know the hope to which He has called you, the riches of His glorious inheritance in His holy people, and His incomparably great power for us who believe.

(Ephesians 1:17-19)

HEAVENS STOREHOUSE
Creative Miracles Department

in EPHESIANS 1: 3-4

the Bible reads:

"Blessed be the God and Father of our Lord Jesus Christ, who hath blessed us with **[how much?]** all spiritual blessings **[where?]** in heavenly places in Christ: according as He hath chosen us in Him before the foundation of the world, that we should be holy and without blame before Him in love."

One of the key parts of this scripture is the tense in which it has been written. It has already taken place. It's already done. When were your blessings put there? Before the foundation of the world. When were you chosen? Before the foundation of the world.

The Living Bible Says in PSALM 139:16

"You saw me before I was born and scheduled each day of my life before I began to breathe. Every day was recorded in Your book."

Our Father has already seen the end and laid it out. He once said that if we follow Him, we will find rich treasure on His path.

He knows where all the treasure is because He has already walked that way. God cares about you! He is interested in every aspect of your life, and He wants you to have the very best life here on earth. Nothing missing and nothing lacking.

A MAN BY THE NAME OF SHAWN BOLZ

wrote a book where he was transported to heaven and taken to a huge warehouse. It was so vast that he could not find the room's perimeters. He couldn't distinguish the ceilings or walls, the structure was so immense.
This is an extract from his book:

"An angel who oversaw the storehouse was assigned to show me around. 'What is this place?' I asked. His eyes lit up. He smiled and replied, 'This is the storehouse of heaven. Every provision that will ever be needed in this age for Jesus to receive the fullness of His inheritance is here, ready and waiting for those who would partner with Him and call it forth.'"

He saw different departments:
- The Department of Creative Miracles
- Heavenly Manna
- Rooms of Divine Architecture
- The Creative Invention Section
- Heaven's music storeroom…
  clothing, farming, and education with creative teaching.

This vision shows the vast abundance of provision that God has provided for us. Everything we will ever need in our lifetime has already been provided for. The inheritance that Jesus recovered for us cannot be received naturally. It must be received by faith, through the Spirit of God.

However, as it is written in 1 Corinthians 2: 9-14

"What no (natural) eye has seen,
   what no (natural) ear has heard,
and what no human mind has conceived"—
   the things God has prepared (prearranged) for those who love him—
these are the things God has revealed to us by His Spirit.

The Spirit searches all things, even the deep things of God. For who knows a person's thoughts except for their own spirit within them? In the same way, no one knows the thoughts of God except the Spirit of God. What we have received is not the spirit of the world, but the Spirit who is from God, so that we may understand what God has freely given us.

This is what we speak, not in words taught us by human wisdom but in words taught by the Spirit, explaining spiritual realities with Spirit-taught words. The person without the Spirit does not accept the things that come from the Spirit of God but considers them foolishness, and cannot understand them because they are discerned only through the Spirit.

IN ETERNITY THERE IS NO SPACE

In the Kingdom there is NO SPACE,
NO MATTER, NO DISTANCE.
Everything is in a spiritual form.

Then Jesus asked him,
"What is your name?"
Mark 5:1-9

"My name is Legion," he replied,
"for we are many."

What is a legion?
A division of 3000-6000 men.

DID YOU KNOW?

HEAVEN IS NON-DIMENSIONAL

IT CANNOT BE MEASURED IN DISTANCE

day night summer winter autumn spring yesterday today tomorrow day night summer winter autumn sprin

IN ETERNITY THERE IS
NO TIME
EVERYTHING IS NOW

"1000 years is one day and one day is as a thousand"

2 Peter 3 v 8

day night summer winter autumn spring yesterday today tomorrow day night summer winter autumn sprin

WHO IS GOD AND WHAT IS GOD?
GOD, OUR MODEL

In Genesis 1:1 we read, "In the beginning God created the heavens and the earth."

He is creating things with words, "calling things" and repositioning things using the power of his words. Now for us to understand God as our model for a life of abundance here on earth, we need to understand who God is, and who He is not. We cannot understand the supernatural unless we understand where it originates from and how we can properly apply it in the "now."

Firstly, we know that according to Numbers 23:19...

GOD IS NOT A MAN. PERIOD.

Secondly, we read in Exodus 3:14, during a dialogue with Moses, God refers to Himself as "I AM". What does this tell us about God?

He IS the self-existent one that doesn't need anything or anybody to exist. God is the one that created everything and doesn't need you, or me, or anything to continue to exist.

So God is not a man...

NOW THE PROBLEM IS, MOST PEOPLE ACKNOWLEDGE THAT GOD IS GOD, BUT ACT AS THOUGH HE WERE A MAN. WHEN WE DO THIS, WHEN WE BELIEVE GOD IS A MAN, WE APPLY ALL THE LAWS THAT APPLY TO US (SPACE, TIME, LIMITATIONS) TO GOD.

Without the supernatural, we are bound to time, distance and the laws of nature. But if we believe God to be the great "I AM" then this means that none of the natural laws apply to Him. When we think God is a man, we put limits on what He can do in our minds, leading us to think thoughts such as "it's going to take too long," or "that could never happen," because subconsciously we are binding God to these human laws.

For example, you sign a contract with the bank that you are going to pay off your bond in 30 years' time, that's the law OR you can choose to believe that your God can operate outside of those laws, paying off your bond in 10 years, 5 years or 30 days! God can pay off that bond right now!

God doesn't exist in the realm of the natural. He exists in the Spirit realm or the supernatural. It's another dimension which cannot be measured in distance.

"Supernatural" by definition is, "a manifestation or event attributed to some force beyond scientific understanding or the laws of nature. (Oxford Languages)

When we break it up, "super" refers to "above and beyond" and "natural" refers to creation or nature. Therefore, "supernatural" can be defined as above and beyond the natural world.

SO GOD IS TRULY ABOVE AND BEYOND.

Above and beyond science
Above and beyond reason
Above and beyond the laws of nature
Above and beyond education
Above and beyond doctors reports

When you move into the supernatural realm, things are accelerated. This practically means things that would normally take years to do in the natural, can be accelerated in the spirit when we do them God's way.

The natural, on the other hand, is the supernatural deaccelerated.

WITH FAITH, WE CAN OVERRIDE TIME.

An example of this that we can find in the Bible is the story of Jesus turning water into wine at a wedding in the village of Cana (John 2:1-11). Jesus was able to produce the wine immediately. He took the time and the toil out of the process, from the harvesting to the crushing of the grapes. He produced the best wine out of heaven's vineyards and he was able to do it in an instant.

"When evening came, his disciples went down to the lake, where they got into a boat and set off across the lake for Capernaum. By now it was dark, and Jesus had not yet joined them. A strong wind was blowing and the waters grew rough. When they had rowed about three or four miles, they saw Jesus approaching the boat, walking on the water; and they were frightened. But he said to them, "It is I; don't be afraid." Then they were willing to take him into the boat, and **immediately** the boat reached the shore where they were heading." *John 6:16-21*

"The days are coming," declares the Lord, "when the **reaper will be overtaken by the plowman** and the planter by the one treading grapes. New wine will drip from the mountains and flow from all the hills, and I will bring my people Israel back from exile. "They will rebuild the ruined cities and live in them. They will plant vineyards and drink their wine; they will make gardens and eat their fruit. I will plant Israel in their own land, never again to be uprooted from the land I have given them," says the Lord your God. *Amos 9:13-15*

JESUS, OUR MODEL

Jesus is also our model. Although Jesus is fully God, He was also a man. God become flesh and lived amongst us. He did this to model how humanity, created in God's image, can do even greater works than Him.

"I TELL YOU THE TRUTH, ANYONE WHO BELIEVES IN ME WILL DO THE SAME WORKS I HAVE DONE, AND EVEN GREATER WORKS, BECAUSE I AM GOING TO BE WITH THE FATHER." JOHN 14:12

JESUS HEALED THE MAIMED

And great multitudes came unto him, having with them those that were lame, blind, dumb, maimed, and many others, and cast them down at Jesus' feet; and he healed them.
Matthew 15:30

Maimed def: wound or injure (a person or animal) so that part of the body is permanently damaged.

QUESTION: WHERE DID HE GET THE PARTS FROM TO FIX THEM?

Heaven's warehouse.

JESUS CREATES FISH LIKE HIS FATHER IN GENESIS 1:20

One day, as the crowds were pressing close to him to hear the word of God, Jesus was standing by the lake of Gennesaret. (THE GARDEN OF A PRINCE)

"He saw two boats moored by the land; the fishermen had gone ashore and were washing their nets. He got into one of the boats - it was Simon's - and asked him to put out a little way from the land. Then he sat down in the boat and began to teach the crowd. When he had finished speaking. he said to Simon, "now go out where its deeper and let down your nets and you will catch a lot of fish!" 'Master, replied Simon, we were working hard all night and caught nothing at all. But if you say so, I'll let down the nets.' When they did so, they caught such a huge number of fish that their nets began to break.

They signalled to their partners in the other boat to come and help them. So they came, and filled both the boats. and they began to sink. When Simon Peter saw it, he fell down at Jesus' knees. "Go away,' he said. 'Leave me, Lord! I'm a sinner!'

JESUS UNLOCKS HEAVENS BEST VINEYARDS

Jesus is bridging the heavens and the earth.

He is standing between 2 realms, the unseen and the seen, the spirit and the flesh.

They have a problem on the earth, they have no wine. He turns water into wine but not just any wine, **the best wine.**

How? Without even owning a vineyard? No equipment?

THE BEST VINEYARDS ARE IN HEAVEN, WHERE THERE IS NO TIME.

He unlocks heaven on earth.

JESUS FEEDS 5000 MEN FROM HEAVEN'S KITCHEN.

Let's look at John 6:4-10 and Matthew 14:18.

And He commanded the crowds to sit down on the grass, and took the five loaves, and the two fishes, and looking up to heaven, He blessed, and broke the loaves to the disciples, and the disciples gave to the people.

KEYS:

Looking up to heaven, trusting ONLY in God.
Psalm 65:2, Jeremiah 17:5-7

Jesus Blessed.
He Releases the Blessing on the loaves and fishes.

Now the question is:

WHERE DID HE GET THE BREAD AND FISH FROM?

Heaven's Kitchen - It's on Reserve. This was on a mountain, NO Food, NO Stores, Nothing.

ONLY THE BLESSING CAN DO THIS!

When God creates, He uses the Blessing, which is the name God gave to the POWER He used to create the universe.

HAVING FAITH IN THE BLESSING

You must understand, what it is, what it does and how to keep it flowing in your life…

WHAT IS THE BLESSING?

The Blessing is the Covenant of God that overrides the curse. It's the Anointing of God through which divine favour flows. It's the Power of God to produce. The Blessing is the presence of God in a person's life that enables them to prosper in every area of their life, regardless of natural circumstances.

It's a **divine enablement** that doesn't care what things look like in the natural. It comes from the Hebrew word *"Baraka"*, meaning *"to bless"*. It means empowerment, it means to endue with power for success in every area of life! You just need to recognize it and have faith.

WHY IS THE BLESSING SO IMPORTANT?

Because God is going to use you to change the economy of a nation and you can't do this without the proficiency, high degree of skill or expertise of the Blessing. The Blessing knows exactly what to do.

THERE IS ONE BLESSING BUT MANY BLESSINGS OF 'THE BLESSING.'

THE BLESSING BRINGS:

Protection
Abraham & Sarah — Genesis 20:3-7

Recompense
Abraham was paid damages, 1000 pieces of silver — Genesis 20:14-16

Wisdom and Witty Ideas
Genesis 47:14-15

Promotions
Joseph — Genesis 41:40-41; Daniel remained relevant for 65 years — Daniel 6:2-3, 28

Inventions and Strategy
Uzziah invented engines — 2 Chronicles 26:15

Real Estate
Ruth — Boazs' Fields — Deuteronomy 6:11

Health & Vitality
What ever the need — 2 Corinthians 9:8

Preservation, Longevity, Fruitfulness
Abraham & Sarah

Strategic Positioning
Joseph in the pit — Gensis 37:24; Peter in the boat

Acceleration, Growth & Development for you and others
Acceleration — Amos 9; Peter 'Marked of God' — Luke 5; Genesis 12:2

Exceptional Business Savvy and Leadership Skills
Jacob flocks increase — Genesis 30:25-43, 31:1

The Blessing will raise you to the top
Deuteronomy 28:1-3 — Job became the greatest businessman in all the east

Isaac sowed in the land, and reaped in the same year a hundredfold — Genesis 26:12

HEBREW:
BARAKA
TO BLESS

THIS BLESSING IS SO POWERFUL, IT HAS THE ABILITY TO REPRODUCE THE GARDEN OF EDEN WHEREVER IT GOES.

That's why you want to paint your house. That's why you want to wash your car.

WHY?

THE BLESSING WANTS TO DO GOOD. THE BLESSING IS PROGRAMMED TO TURN EVERY DESOLATE PLACE INTO THE GARDEN OF EDEN.

WHAT WILL THE BLESSING DO?

Anything you desire within the constraints of the Word.

It's purpose is to provide you with power for success in every area of your life.

Proverbs 10:22 NIV
The blessing of the LORD brings wealth.

2 Corinthians 9:8 AMP
And God [I AM] is able to make all grace [every favour and earthly blessing] come in abundance to you, so that you may always [under all circumstances, regardless of the need] [WHATEVER THE NEED] have complete sufficiency in everything [being completely self-sufficient in Him], and have an abundance for every good work and act of charity.

Deuteronomy 28:2 ESV
And all these blessings shall come upon you and overtake you, if you obey the voice of the LORD your God.

Your part is just to have faith in the Blessing! You may say, "This is our budget" or "This is our price range." The Blessing doesn't care, it will deliver what you want.

In the story in Luke 5:1-10, we see the Blessing in action.

THE BLESSING HAS NO RESPECT FOR AMOUNT. IT DOESN'T CARE ABOUT TIME, SEASONS, AMOUNTS, DOCTORS' REPORTS, PROFESSIONAL OPINIONS, OR PEOPLE'S OPINIONS.

Jesus was standing by the Lake of Gennesaret and people were listening to Him teach the word of God. Jesus noticed the boats, one belonging to Simon Peter, and asked him to take the boat a little further out. After teaching for a while, Jesus encouraged Simon to let down his nets, to which he replied, "Master, we've worked hard all night and haven't caught anything.
But because you say so, I will let down the nets."

Immediately, such a large number of fish came into the nets that the boats themselves began to sink! The Blessing was on Jesus, and every fish in that lake made its way to Him. The Blessing that Jesus taught on that day didn't care if there were fish or not, it created more. How? Because that's what it can do!

WHATEVER THE NEED.

The Blessing will override all natural laws and create the garden of Eden because it has built into it's DNA the power to:

RENEW
RESTORE
REVIVE
REFRESH

It's the power of God that was used to create the universe, including all the fish in the sea, right at the beginning.

THE FIRST MENTION OF THE BLESSING

In Genesis 1:28 it looks like God is communicating with Adam, but He's not. He's actually transferring power. He's transferring His creative power.

Then God said, "Let us make man in our image, after our likeness. And let them have dominion over the fish of the sea and over the birds of the heavens and over the livestock and over all the earth and over every creeping thing that creeps on the earth." So God created man in His own image, in the image of God He created him; male and female He created them. Genesis 1:26-27 ESV

In Genesis 2:7, God then tells us, in more detail, about the creation of this first human being, "And the LORD God formed man of the dust of the ground, and breathed into his nostrils the breath of life; and man became a living soul." (KJV)

And so Adam was created — an extraordinary birth out of clay, with God's breath in his body. Now Adam didn't hear those first words God spoke to him because he wasn't yet alive. But once those words entered him, they did their creative work and, as the Bible says,

"MAN BECAME A SPEAKING SPIRIT LIKE GOD"
Chumash (Gen 2:7)

ADAM WAS EXACTLY LIKE GOD,

not just a part of Him, he was absolutely filled with God. Born of God's word, Adam was love, just as God is love. Adam was full of compassion, just as God is full of compassion. The only difference that existed was that while God is eternally sovereign and independent, man was created to be totally dependent on God.

And God blessed them. And God said to them, **"Be fruitful and multiply and fill the earth and subdue it, and have dominion over the fish of the sea and over the birds of the heavens and over every living thing that moves on the earth."** (Genesis 1:28 ESV)

This verse tells that God Almighty staggeringly crowns this first human family with honour and glory and the responsibility to have dominion over all creation.

This fact is so well articulated in Psalm 8.

This blessing marks the beginning of the human story, the first words that Adam ever heard. God wasn't communicating with Adam, He was transferring His creative power, empowering him with the power of the Blessing.

As a living, speaking spirit like God, man had the same power to speak that God Himself had. He was full of God's own faith and had the authority to speak creative, compassionate words and exercise dominion with them.

As a result, we see Adam operating in the Garden of Eden as an extraordinary being, walking around the garden without any fear. God brings all the animals to Adam who then names them all—an amazing feat of intelligence.

He names every animal one by one and remembers them all. This is Adam. This is you. Why? Because inside of Adam was dominion power and authority.

When God put Adam in the garden He gave him an assignment to dress it and keep it. He was to take this 'Blessing' and make the earth be fruitful, make it produce, multiply it, expand it, replenish it, means to perpetually renew and supply it, or stock it with abundance or fulfil former fulness in this earth. He was to take the garden and everywhere he went, he was to produce the garden with the power of the Blessing.

We all know what happens next, Adam disobeys God and is deceived by the devil, eating fruit from the tree of good and evil.

We see God's response in Genesis 3:17, and the curse enters humanity;

"Because you listened to your wife and ate fruit from the tree about which I commanded you, 'You must not eat from it,' Cursed is the ground because of you; through painful toil you will eat food from it all the days of your life." (NIV)

"MAN BECAME A SPEAKING SPIRIT LIKE GOD"

JESUS RECOVERS OUR CROWN

Jesus came and recovered our crown, taking the curse for us with His death on the cross and recovering the Blessing, that we might receive the promise of the Spirit through faith.
(See Galatians 3:13-14)

God's original plan before the fall, that we would be fruitful, multiply and replenish the Earth has not changed. With Jesus and the power of the Blessing, this is possible.

AGAIN, WHY IS THE BLESSING SO IMPORTANT?

Because God is leading you to a piece of property you can't afford. He's leading you into a battle you can't win so that He can prove He's God all by Himself. That building you are wanting to build; if you could do it alone, it's not faith.

He's taking you there on purpose.

Now some people walk around their whole life with this Blessing but never access the power hidden in it. Why? They don't have faith in it or they may not know they even have it.

Jacob needed a way to take the time and the toil out of every situation, so he leaned on the Blessing, which is designed to override all natural laws.

When you are dealing with the Blessing you have an ultimate edge above all your competitors because you are dealing with God and none of the natural laws apply to Him. God is not a man (Numbers 11) therefore all the laws that apply to man do not apply to Him. He is above and beyond natural laws. The Blessing operates outside of natural law. Whatever the need, the Blessing doesn't care how big the need or desire, the Blessing knows what to do.

That's why you can put a piece of property before it at 10 Million, 100 million, because it doesn't care, it has no respect for any amount. That's why He says, whatsoever things you desire (no matter the size) when you pray, BELIEVE, rest on the Blessing to do it and you shall have it (Mark 11:24).

The state of the economy doesn't matter, because the Blessing will still provide plenty even in a famine. The economy of heaven is always up, which is why He says in the days of famine you shall be satisfied. (Psalm 37:19).

2 Corinthians 9 verse 8 tells us that God is able " to make every grace overflow to you."

You don't have to put in the effort and strain. The Blessing knows what to do!

LEARN TO LEAN ON THE BLESSING.

If we look at Jacob's life, the Blessing was on him but he didn't use it for 20 years while working for Laban.
This blessing will get you anything you desire without painful toil, that's the miracle. When we're in Him, anything is possible. God is totally self-sufficient. He doesn't need people or the world to accomplish His purposes. He can do it all by Himself.

Proverbs 10:22 (KJV) puts it this way;

> "THE BLESSING OF THE LORD, IT MAKETH RICH, AND HE ADDETH NO SORROW WITH IT."

HOW YOU CAN EXPERIENCE THE BLESSING?

The simple answer is that the Blessing will come upon you and overtake you **IF** you obey the voice of the Lord your God.

UNLESS YOU ARE BORN AGAIN YOU CANNOT SEE THE KINGDOM OF GOD.

You may ask, "Well how do operate as God intended for me to operate? How do I access all that God has provided for me?"

This is your personal invitation from the Father:
"I have come that you may have life and have it more abundantly!" John 10:10

Part of Jesus' commission was the recovery of sight for the blind. Jesus wants to invite you to be a part of His glorious kingdom. Your eyes can be opened to see and receive all that God has prepared for you. John 3:3 says: "Except a man be born again he cannot see the kingdom of God."

For you to operate in this spiritual realm you need to accept Jesus as Lord and Saviour of your life.

He wants to invite you back home today! Romans 5:17: "For if because of one man's trespass (lapse, offence) death reigned through that one, much more surely will those who receive [God's] overflowing grace (unmerited favour) and the free gift of righteousness [putting them into right standing with himself] reign as kings in life through the one man Jesus Christ (the Messiah, the anointed one)."

We want to invite you to say this prayer with us in all sincerity and confidence:

WRITE DOWN YOUR NAME AND THE DATE YOU ACCEPTED THE INVITATION.

INVITATION

Lord Jesus, I believe in you. Thank you for giving your life for me. Thank you for taking my sin + shame upon the cross. I need you... I need your grace to forgive me, and I need your love to change me. Thank you for your amazing love! I accept you as my Lord + Saviour. Come into my heart now.

I am saved, and that means you live in me. I belong to you.

In Jesus name, Amen!

Name
Date:

CONGRATULATIONS!

This is how God sees you...

By accepting Jesus as Lord and Saviour of your life, you have been translated out of the kingdom of darkness into the kingdom of light (Colossians 1:3).

God has purchased you with the precious blood of His own Son. He has adopted you into His royal family and He wants you to live and reflect Him in all His glory and splendor. That's why you are called a royal priesthood, a holy nation, a people for God's own possession: that we may show the excellency of Him who has called you out of darkness into His marvelous light (1 Peter 2:9).

Seeing yourself this way is so important. You cannot talk or act like a king until you see yourself as a king! Satan's power and dominion was broken over 2000 years ago. When Jesus laid His life down for you and me, there was a beautiful exchange.

Jesus took upon Himself every curse (sickness, poverty, and death) for you and for me, and left the blessing (Galatians 3:13 - 14). He took your life and gave you His life! He became poor, so that we might be eternally rich.

You now have the same DNA structure as the Father, and His divine nature because of the commitment you have just made! You are hooked up with the possessor of heaven and earth. The unlimited power source! That's why nothing is impossible for you.

Let me paint a new picture of who you are because of your new commitment!

THIS IS THE TRUTH.

THE TRUTH

You are not ordinary. You are God's crowning glory and He loves you.

You are a peculiar treasure to God. You are treasured in the throne rooms of heaven. You are the apple of His eye. You have been chosen for this very hour, separated and set apart for sacred use. You were created to reflect God's glory in the earth. You were created to stand out and shine in this world of darkness. You are the custodians of light, the distributers of eternal life. You hold all the treasures of wisdom and knowledge. You have within you the answer to every problem. God sees you as a ruler. He sees you rich. He sees you as a joint heir with Jesus. He sees you as the righteousness of God. Isn't it exciting to know that you have God on your side working all things for your good!

YOU ARE NOT ORDINARY ANYMORE. YOU ARE GOD'S CROWNING GLORY!

AND THEN
GOD CREATED MAN

So God created man in **His own image**; in the image of God He created him; male and female He created them. Then God **blessed them**, and God said to them, "Be fruitful and multiply; fill the earth and subdue it; have **dominion** over the fish of the sea, over the birds of the air, and over every living thing that moves on the earth.

GENESIS 1:27-28

Then the Lord God formed man from the dust of the ground and **breathed** into his nostrils the breath or **spirit of life**, and man became a living being.

GENESIS 2:7

"WHY WOULD YOU BOTHER WITH PUNY, MORTAL MAN OR CARE ABOUT HUMAN BEINGS? YET WHAT HONOR YOU HAVE GIVEN TO MEN, CREATED ONLY A LITTLE LOWER THAN ELOHIM, CROWNED WITH GLORY AND MAGNIFICENCE. YOU HAVE DELEGATED TO THEM **RULERSHIP** OVER ALL YOU HAVE MADE, WITH EVERYTHING UNDER THEIR AUTHORITY, PLACING EARTH ITSELF UNDER THE FEET OF YOUR **IMAGE-BEARERS**."

PSALM 8:4-6

AND SO, ADAM, MADE IN GOD'S IMAGE, NAMED THE ANIMALS, JUST LIKE HIS FATHER!

GENESIS 2:20

"And Adam gave names to all cattle, and to the fowl of the air, and to every beast of the field.."

NOW IT'S YOUR TURN

Now that we've gained an understanding of this incredible inheritance that Jesus has recovered for us, we need to look at the practical steps that need to be taken to receive this inheritance, by faith, through the Spirit of God.

We're going to share six steps with you that have been tried and tested to bring forth your dreams and desires. We encourage you to prayerfully complete these steps and watch all that God will do in and through you!

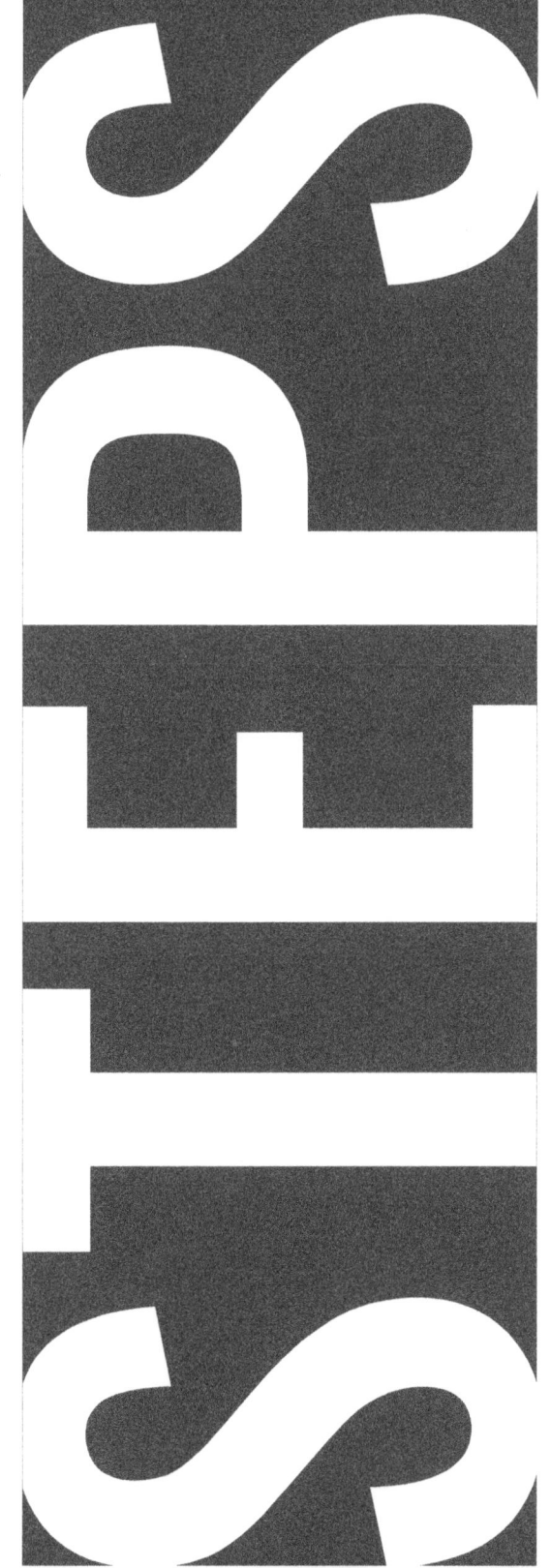

STEP 1:

TAKE TIME TO WRITE DOWN YOUR DREAM.

The more detail, the better. What is your greatest desire? What would you like to accomplish more than anything else in your life? What would you attempt to do if you knew it was impossible to fail?

Be inspired by these scriptures:

Psalm 37:4, Proverbs 10:27, Ephesians 3:20 Amp, Proverbs 23:7, Jeremiah 17: 5-8, Luke 16:19-22

STEP 2:

MEDATATION ON GOD'S "UNFAILING" WORD ESTABLISHES A FIRM FOUNDATION.

Gather as many promises of God as you can (we call these promises the "seed") which pertain to your dream. God's word is the visual image, a picture of the desired result. It is the heavenly sustenance (**the upholding power**) by which you begin the construction of your dream.

Matthew 9:27-30
We must believe and have faith that the Lord can do what we're asking of Him.

Proverbs 24:13-14, Numbers 23:19, Psalm 138:2, John 1:1-3, Joshua 1:8, Psalm 1:2-3, Psalm 119:130

STEP 3:

GET THE DETAIL DOWN. FAITH NEEDS A TARGET! BE SPECIFIC!

If a carpenter asked you, "What type of coffee table would you like?" Your answer would need to be specific and not "Anything!" or "I don't mind..."
Would you prefer glass, wood, or plastic? Chrome legs or steel?

Luke 18:35-43, Matthew 20:20-21

Count the cost (Luke 14:28) but trust that the Lord is your source of provision.

STEP 4:

START BUILDING YOUR DREAM. CREATING FAITH PROPS. THE CLEARER THE PICTURE THE FASTER THE DELIVERY!
Jeremiah 1:11-12

Get pictures or anything that relates to your dream. If you have a dream to build or renovate a house, source pictures of what you would like your house to look like, what colour paint, flooring etc.

Habakkuk 2:2, Genesis 11:6, Genesis 15:3-5, Acts 10, Genesis 30:25-43, Genesis 31:10-12.

STEP 5:

DECLARING THE END RESULT. SPEAK THE WORD OVER YOUR DREAM!

Matthew 8:6-10, Rev 19:11-16
Ecc 9:4, Psalm 103:20-21, Psalm 35:27

ENGAGE THE POWERFUL CREATIVE FORCE OF THE TONGUE

Proverbs 4:23, Habakkuk 2:2-3

You were made in God's image and able to operate in His likeness (Genesis 1:26). In the beginning God called forth light, although there was darkness! He didn't focus on the darkness, He only focused on the end result—light. Stop looking at your current circumstances! Call forth your dream (confessing the 'meditated seed' daily until you witness the manifestation), and declare the end result from the beginning (Isaiah 46:10).
As children of the Most High, we have a right to call 'things' that be not as though they are (Romans 4:17).

Start today, come into agreement with His unfailing word (His 'seed') and watch 'it' work!

STEP 6:

LET YOUR LIFE TESTIFY OF HIS GOODNESS AND THANK HIM FOR IT.

EXPERIENCE THE WONDERS OF GIVING GOD PRAISE...

Give God all praise for bringing your dream to pass.
The Word says in Revelations 12:11, "They overcame by the blood of the lamb and the word of their testimony."
Matthew 5:14-16, 1 Peter 2:9

BY GIVING GOD PRAISE, YOU ARE INVITING THE ALMIGHTY TO STEP INTO YOUR SITUATION.
2 Chronicles 20-12, 15, 17-25; Acts 16:25-26

01

TAKE TIME TO WRITE DOWN YOUR DREAM

STEP ONE

THE MORE DETAIL, THE BETTER. WHAT IS YOUR GREATEST DESIRE? WHAT WOULD YOU LIKE TO ACCOMPLISH MORE THAN ANYTHING ELSE IN YOUR LIFE? WHAT WOULD YOU ATTEMPT TO DO IF YOU KNEW IT WAS IMPOSSIBLE TO FAIL?

PSALM 37:4, PROVERBS 10:27, EPHESIANS 3:20 AMP, PROVERBS 23:7, JEREMIAH 17:5-8, LUKE 16:19-22

Imagine that the pen in your hand is a golden miracle wand and it's been handed to you by your creator.

HE SAYS TO YOU, "WHATEVER YOU WRITE IN THIS DREAM BOOK WILL APPEAR IN YOUR LIFETIME."

He wants you to dream without limits.

What is your greatest desire? What would you like to accomplish more than anything else in your life? Have you ever thought about it? What would you attempt to do if you knew it was impossible to fail?

DREAM WITHOUT LIMITS AND DREAM UNRESTRAINED.

Write down everything that you desire. Do you want to write a book? Is there a special person you would like to meet? Is there a specific business opportunity you would like to get involved in? Do you hate being overweight? If so, what would your desired goal weight be? It's important to note that this principle can work for you or against you.

When we first started doing this exercise of writing down dreams with a youth group, a particular young girl didn't take this exercise seriously. On her 'dream sheet', she listed hot steamy nights, nights out on the town, drinking etc. Fast forward a few years down the line and she had received exactly what she had asked for. She received what she desired —her life was a mess. Two other girls from the same youth group dreamed of great marks to excel academically. The Holy Spirit helped them and He imparted to them a spirit of excellence and made them of quick understanding. With His help, they became top of their class. One was awarded Dux and one excelled in accountancy. Both received bursaries.

When aligned with His will, God will give you the desires of your heart. According to Proverbs 4:23, everything we do flows from our hearts. In other words, your life is produced from the 'inside out'. First, it comes through your spirit, then the physical. Your external circumstances are a physical manifestation of what is happening in the spirit realm.

A GOOD STORY TO ILLUSTRATE THIS POINT IS THAT OF LAZARUS.

There once lived a rich man clothed in purple and fine linen who fared sumptuously every day. There was a beggar named Lazarus who desired the crumbs that fell from the rich man's table. He was full of sores, and the dogs came and licked his sores.

Eventually, the beggar died and was carried by angels into Abraham's bosom. The rich man also died and was buried. Notice that the beggar was saved because the angels took him into Abrahams's bosom (Luke 16:19-31).

But he was broke, he was sick and he was immobile. What did the beggar desire? Crumbs! Remember, "God will give you the desires of your heart." (Psalm 37:4)

THINK BIG

IF YOU DESIRE CRUMBS YOU'LL GET CRUMBS

THE KEY TAKEAWAY:
When you are writing down your dreams, don't desire crumbs. Desire the very finest that God has for you. You are His children and He loves you. This is not about need, this is about want.

It gives God pleasure that you get the best. He's like a father who loves to spoil His children. The Bible says that He takes pleasure in your prosperity (Psalm 35:27).

Some people don't believe in divine healing. But, that does not mean it is not available to you. **God will leave you in a place because He will not violate your will.**

Matthew 9:27-29 (NIV) says,
As Jesus went on from there, two blind men followed Him, calling out, "Have mercy on us, Son of David!"
When He had gone indoors, the blind men came to Him, and He asked them, "Do you believe that I am able to do this?" "Yes, Lord," they replied. Then He touched their eyes and said, "According to your faith let it be done to you."

BE CAREFUL OF THE DESIRES OF YOUR HEART...

"Now to Him Who, by (in consequence of) the [action of His] power that is at work within us, is able to [carry out His purpose and] do superabundantly, far over and above all that we [dare] ask or think. [infinitely beyond our highest prayers, desires, thoughts, hopes, or dreams]." Ephesians 3:20 AMPC

The same power that raised Jesus from the dead is the same power that is working in you, able to carry out its purpose and do abundantly, far beyond what we dare ask or think.

You cannot outdream God — He is too big!

DON'T PUT LIMITATIONS OF TIME, MAN OR MONEY ON YOUR DREAMS.

Don't look at what you have, look at what He has! He has it, and it is for you.
God doesn't give you a dream and then expects you to pay for it. Where there is vision there is provision.

One of the tricks of the enemy is to convince you to connect your income with how far you can go. "This is my income, this is all I can do." No, it's a trick.
Don't look at what's in your hands. Look at what is in His hands.

PROVERBS 23:7
"AS A MAN THINKETH IN HIS HEART SO IS HE..."

MEDITATION ON GOD'S "UNFAILING" WORD ESTABLISHES A FIRM FOUNDATION.

STEP TWO

GATHER AS MANY PROMISES OF GOD AS YOU CAN (WE CALL THESE PROMISES THE "SEED") WHICH PERTAIN TO YOUR DREAM. GOD'S WORD IS THE VISUAL IMAGE, A PICTURE OF THE DESIRED RESULT. IT IS THE HEAVENLY SUSTENANCE (THE UPHOLDING POWER) BY WHICH YOU BEGIN THE CONSTRUCTION OF YOUR DREAM.

MATTHEW 9:27-30 (WE MUST BELIEVE AND HAVE FAITH THAT THE LORD CAN DO WHAT WE'RE ASKING OF HIM).

PROVERBS 24:13-14, NUMBERS 23:19, PSALM 138:2, JOHN 1:1-3, JOSHUA 1:8, PSALM 1:2-3, PSALM 119:130

MEDITATION ON GODS "UNFAILING" WORD ESTABLISHES A FIRM FOUNDATION.

Establishing a firm foundation is aligning your dream with God's Word. He will uphold it, He will watch over it, and He will make it good (Numbers 23: 19).
You don't have to be concerned about how it's going to happen. One of the examples we use is a watch.
We are really not interested in how the watch came about, the stainless steel, and the little bits and bobs, the hands, and how it all came together in the factory. We're only interested in the final product. What goes on behind the scenes is irrelevant.

Your part is to align your dream with God's Word and believe that what He said He will do, He will do. His part is to make it good. His Word is forever settled in heaven (Psalm 119:89). God cannot lie or deny Himself (2 Timothy 2:17), and the scriptures cannot be broken (John 13:35).

GOD'S WORD IS A PICTURE OF THE DESIRED RESULT.

Everything that is in the invisible realm, the **Bible** has a picture of it. God has made it so that you can **see with the eyes of faith** through the Word (Psalm 119:130). When you can **see it**, **light enters your heart** and something happens inside. When you align your dream with God's Word there's a confidence, there's an assurance and there's **peace**.

Meditation on God's Word brings revelation or advanced knowledge, which puts you at peace. Let me show you the story of Gehazi from 2 Kings 6:14 - 17.

"Therefore he sent horses and chariots and a great army there, and they came by night and surrounded the city. And when the servant of the man of God arose early and went out, there was an army, surrounding the city with horses and chariots. And his servant said to him, "Alas, my master! What shall we do?" So he answered, "Do not fear, for those who are with us are more than those who are with them." And Elisha prayed, and said, "LORD, I pray, open his eyes that he may see." Then the LORD opened the eyes of the young man, and he saw. And behold, the mountain was full of horses and chariots of fire all around Elisha."

Gehazi was fearful because he saw only with his natural eyes. He was being moved by what he saw in the physical! But, Elisha was not moved by what he saw in the natural because he had a revelation or advanced knowledge of a great army which was unseen to the natural eye. Elisha saw into the spiritual realm with the eye of faith. He saw the real situation. The mountain was full of horses and chariots of fire all around, and he was at peace.

Let me give you a practical example of a scripture I meditate all the time that goes like this:

"Father I thank you for bringing me to a land full of good things, for giving me great and good cities which I did not build and houses full of good things which I did not fill. Wells dug out which I did not dig, and vineyards and olive trees which I did not plant. When I have enough food to make me I'm full, I will not forget you Lord."
Deut. 6:10-11

What is in houses full of good things? Everything, including a beautiful car in the garage. What are wells you never dug?

Opportunities and financial surprises you never looked for. Somebody is digging the wells for you. This is a foundation seed. If you want to have a house full of good things, you would write this scripture in your Dream Book Journal as your foundation seed, and meditate on it until light arises in your heart, and your faith comes alive.

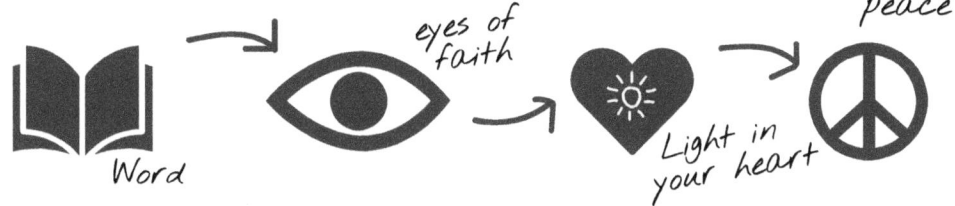

GOD'S WORD IS THE HEAVENLY SUSTENANCE, THE UPHOLDING POWER BY WHICH YOU BEGIN THE CONSTRUCTION OF YOUR DREAM.

Hebrews 1:3 "He will uphold all things by the word of His power."

Everything, including your car, your house, and your business is upheld by the word of His power.

Every brick of your house is upheld by the word of His power.

"In the beginning, there was the Word, and the Word was with God, and the Word was God. All things are made by Him, and without Him there was nothing made that was made." (John 1:1,3)

We used this scripture when we were struggling to have a child: "Nothing was made without Him and His word."

We cried, we prayed, we fasted, and we had words spoken over us. We did everything. We looked in every place for a solution and He took me to this scripture:
"All things are made by Him, and without Him, there was nothing made that was made." John 1:3.
It also says that "He is the Word."

So my wife and I had to feed our hearts with the word to expand our thinking to make our little boy available to us. Our son Ethan was conceived and made manifest on this principle. You have to sow the SEED of the word into your heart. You have to force your heart to produce the result, because "everything flows from it." Plant the word daily until your faith comes alive. When your faith comes alive, God's integrity is at stake, so He rises up to defend it.

FAITH BEGINS WHERE THE WILL OF GOD IS KNOWN, AND FAITH STOPS AT A QUESTION MARK.

Numbers 23:19 "God is not human, that He should lie, not a human being, that He should change His mind. Does He speak and then not act? Does He promise and not fulfill?"

If He said it, He will do it. You have got to believe that. You have to believe it with all your heart. You have to lean totally on the Word. You have to believe everything that He says. When He says He is going to fill a house with good things, He means what He says.

BEING FULLY PERSUADED BY GOD'S UNFAILING WORD IS ESSENTIAL.

If there is any doubt involved, your dream will not come to fruition.
(Look at the story of Abraham in Romans 4:18-21)

So, how do you become fully persuaded? By gathering the promises of God relating to your dream and meditating on them until you prove to yourself that it is God's will for your life and it's what He wants for you.

Against all hope, Abraham in hope **believed** and so became the father of many nations, just as it had been said to him, "So shall your offspring be." Without weakening in his **faith**, he faced the fact that his body was as good as dead—since he was about a hundred years old—and that Sarah's womb was also dead. Yet he **did not waver through unbelief** regarding the promise of God, but was strengthened in his **faith** and gave glory to God, being **fully persuaded** that God had power to do what he had promised.

Romans 4:18-21

HERE ARE A FEW EXAMPLES:

IS IT GOD'S WILL FOR ME TO HAVE ABUNDANCE?

Let's look at what He says about it.

3 John 1:2 (NIV)
"Dear friend, I pray that you may enjoy good health and that all may go well with you, even as your soul is getting along well"

1 Timothy 6:17 (NIV)
Command those who are rich in this present world not to be arrogant nor to put their hope in wealth, which is so uncertain, but to put their hope in God, who richly provides us with everything for our enjoyment.

Deuteronomy 28:8, 11, 12
The Lord will send a blessing on your barns and on everything you put your hand to. The Lord your God will bless you in the land He is giving you. 11 The Lord will grant you abundant prosperity—in the fruit of your womb, the young of your livestock and the crops of your ground—in the land He swore to your ancestors to give you. 12 The Lord will open the heavens, the storehouse of His bounty, to send rain on your land in season and to bless all the work of your hands. You will lend to many nations but will borrow from none.

IS IT GOD'S WILL FOR ME TO HAVE DIVINE HEALTH?

READ PSALM 107:20, AND PROVERBS 4:20-22.

IS IT GOD'S WILL FOR ME TO LIVE FREE FROM FEAR AND WORRY?

READ PSALM 23:4, AND PSALM 91:10-11.

So we fix our eyes not on what is seen, (ie- struggling without money) but on what is unseen (God's blessing of the work of your hands, divine health), since what is seen is temporary (subject to change), but what is unseen (with the natural eye) is eternal.

What is unseen in your life?

It's time to paint new pictures in your heart using the Word of God. The promise of God will bring to nothing your negative circumstances and bring forth your desired result.

As you meditate on the Word a new image begins to grow and take shape in your heart. You begin to see yourself and your circumstances with the eyes of faith.

How can we ensure God's commitment to making our dream a reality?
A covenant is unlike a promise, it is a vow that cannot be broken once the required conditions have been met. There is no force in the kingdom of God stronger than the force of the covenant.

As the covenantor, God's part is always sure and constant, while man has always been the unstable and variable part. God's commitment to His covenant is so strong that He said:

"My covenant I will not break, nor alter the thing that has gone out of my lips." Psalm 89:34.

THE COVENANT IS STRONGER THAN ANY CIRCUMSTANCE.

Nothing can break its efficiency. God's covenant with man is as eternal as day and night.

THE PROMISE?

COVENANT ALIGNMENT
A COMMITMENT TO WALK IN THE TRUTH

God's commitment comes in the form of a covenant which is like a contract that involves two or more people, in this case, between God and His people.

The Bible is loaded with promises from God to make our destinies colourful and enviable on the earth, but certain conditions need to be fulfilled before any of the promises can come to fruition in your life.

Meeting these conditions is what turns the promises into a covenant, and commits God to do His part. Once you locate the covenant demands in any area and meet them, your struggles will be over, and your victory is sure in that area.

"For we can do nothing against the truth but for the truth." 2 Corinthians 13:8

Faith is not waiting for God to work. Faith is putting God's word to work, So as to commit God to make good His promise.

Whatever God tells you to do – do it!

Whatever you are believing God for, ask yourself this question:

AM I WALKING IN THE TRUTH REGARDING THIS SUBJECT?

For instance, you may be saying, "Lord, I'm believing you for peace in my home." Do you really love your wife as Christ loved the Church? (Ephesians 5:25)
Wives, are you subject to your husband? (Ephesians 5: 22)

"Lord I want you to intervene in my finances."
Are you a tither? (Malachai 3:10)
The scriptures cannot be broken, He will not intervene contrary to His word.

"O Lord strengthen me!" (Psalm 84: 7)
"They go from strength to strength everyone in Zion appearing before God."
Are you in church? You may answer , "No, I don't have the time!"
Then you simply don't have time for strength, because it is in Mount Zion that you gain strength.

"Lord I want you to make my children great."
Are you setting a great example? Like father, like son.
God said to Abraham, "I know him that will command his children after him, they will follow in his steps." (Genesis 18:19)

"Lord, why does it feel like everything in my life is a challenge?"
Honor your father and your mother, as the Lord your God commanded you, that your days may be long, and that it may go well with you in the land that the Lord your God is giving you. (Deuteronmy 5:16)

Everything you are asking God for requires your alignment and leaves you with a responsibility.

Are you walking in the truth concerning what you are asking God to do? If you aren't your dream will never become a reality. Faith is not an enchantment. Faith draws its power from the finished work of Christ when you are walking in the truth.

Covenant alignment is essential to making your dreams a reality. Your part has to be played before God's integrity is committed to performing His part.

HIDDEN COVENANTS

GET THE DETAIL DOWN, FAITH NEEDS A TARGET! BE SPECIFIC

STEP THREE

IF A CARPENTER ASKED YOU, "WHAT TYPE OF COFFEE TABLE WOULD YOU LIKE?" YOUR ANSWER WOULD NEED TO BE SPECIFIC, NOT, "ANYTHING!" OR "I DON'T MIND..."
WOULD YOU PREFER GLASS, WOOD, OR PLASTIC? CHROME LEGS OR STEEL?

LUKE 18:35-43, MATTHEW 20:20-21

COUNT THE COST (LUKE 14:28) BUT TRUST THAT THE LORD IS YOUR SOURCE OF PROVISION.

THERE ARE MANY SCRIPTURES WHICH ILLUSTRATE THIS.

Let's look at Mark 10:46-52. In this portion of scripture, you see the story of Blind Bartimaeus. Jesus asked him, **"What do you want?"** Now, Jesus could clearly see that the man was blind, but he still asked this question anyway.

God will not violate your will. What do you want Him to do for you today? What do you want from God? It's available to you. He wants you to be specific. God does not answer vague prayers because faith needs a target.

A great biblical example to look at in this regard is Solomon — the wisest man that ever lived before Jesus's time. Solomon knew both how to plan, and how to be specific.

In 1 Kings 5:6, we see that Solomon was building a temple. He was specific in every single detail, down to the wood and gold that was used and where it would be situated. He stipulated how the angel wings would be spread over the ark of the covenant and the specific size the rooms should be.

EVERY DETAIL MATTERED AND GOD WANTS THE SAME FROM YOU.

Let's take a closer look at the story…

Solomon's first major task is to build the Temple of the Lord. To achieve this architectural feat, Solomon employs professionals from all corners of his kingdom. Three chapters (1 Kings 5-7) are devoted to describing the work of building the Temple, of which we have space only for a small selection:

For some context, Solomon had just taken over as the king of Israel, and Hiram of Tyre sent the ambassadors to extend congratulations and goodwill. (1 Kings 5:1)

Solomon replied with a proposal about the Temple of the Lord he intended to build. (Take note here that Solomon didn't waste any time. His proposal had been planned. He knows exactly where he's going and what he's doing). Solomon asked the king for skilled labourers. They had to arrange how the cedars would be sent as they were cut up river in Lebanon. They had to come down the Mediterranean Sea to meet the high volume to build the temple. They had to prepare rafts of these big trees so they could be transported together down the river. But it took four years just for the preperation and planning. It took another 7 years to build.

"And here is how you can help: Give orders for cedars to be cut from the Lebanon forest; my loggers will work alongside yours and I'll pay your men whatever wage you set. We both know that there is no one like you Sidonians for cutting timber."
(1 Kings 5:6)

1 Kings 5:1 in The Living Bible translation puts it this way:
"And he sent the ambassadors to extend congratulations and goodwill."

Your plans are exceptionally important, down to the last detail. To give an example of how to be specific, let's consider a table. What table would you like? The Lord wants to know. Is it chrome? Is it wood? Is it plastic? You know there are so many different variants of materials that could be used. If it was debt that you were trying to settle, you would gather together the various bills you receive, like a bank home loan, clothing accounts etc. If you're going to settle your debt, you need a target. You need to know who you owe and how much you owe so that faith can go and work towards that target. Get the details down. Another example would be for a partner. Before my wife met me she made a list that went something like this…

LYDIA'S DREAM MAN

I would like a man that is saved and puts God first in his life. A godly man with high values. I would like a good-looking man. A blonde-haired man with blue eyes. A man that is ambitious in business. Driven, romantic, who will love and understand me. Someone who will spoil me, someone I can share with and talk to. He must be clean on himself, clean teeth, breath, clean nails etc… And he must respect me and have a good sense of humour.

So this is the kind of thing you need to to work with, when you're getting down to specifics.

Where does the guy work, what are his hobbies... get specific... get everything down... if you want a job, think how far you want to work from home.

Do you want a company car?

What salary do you want to earn?

Do you want a double pay cheque?

BE SPECIFIC

WHAT DO YOU WANT?

I WANT TO SEE!

04

START BUILDING YOUR DREAM. CREATING FAITH PROPS. THE CLEARER THE PICTURE THE FASTER THE DELIVERY!

Jeremiah 1: 11-12

STEP FOUR

GET PICTURES OR ANYTHING THAT RELATES TO YOUR DREAM. IF YOU HAVE A DREAM TO BUILD OR RENOVATE A HOUSE, SOURCE PICTURES OF WHAT YOU WOULD LIKE YOUR HOUSE TO LOOK LIKE, WHAT COLOUR PAINT, FLOORING ETC.

HABAKKUK 2:2, GENESIS 11:6,
GENESIS 15:3-5, ACTS 10,
GENESIS 30:25-43,
GENESIS 31:10-12.

THE CLEARER THE PICTURE, THE FASTER THE DELIVERY.

Pictures are great faith boosters and powerful triggers of faith.

We see this in the book of Jeremiah chapter 1:11-12 (NIV)

The word of the Lord came to me: "What do you see, Jeremiah?"
"I see the branch of an almond tree," I replied. The Lord said to me, "You have seen correctly, for I am watching to see that my word is fulfilled."

When building your dream sheet, find pictures that relate to your dream. If your dream is to build or renovate a house, find pictures of what you would want your house to look like. What colour paint would you choose? Is it textured? What kind of flooring would you choose? Gather samples of carpet swatches, paint palettes, or kitchen layouts. The clearer the picture, the faster the delivery.

Maybe, like we were, you are believing God for a family. Gather together pictures of your dream theme for your little one's nursery. What type of cot would you like? Get catalogues from baby furniture stores and start building your nursery on paper.

Habakkuk 2:2 says, "Write the vision and engrave it so plainly upon tablets that everyone who passes may (be able to) read it (easily and quickly), as he hastens by."

In this step, we encourage you to create faith props to assist you in keeping your vision constantly before your eyes, as God did with Abraham. These pictures affect your belief system.

TAKE A LOOK AT WHAT GOD DID FOR ABRAHAM:

Genesis 15:3-5 (NIV)
3 And Abram said, "You have given me no children; so a servant in my household will be my heir." 4 Then the word of the Lord came to him: "This man will not be your heir, but a son who is your own flesh and blood will be your heir." 5 He took him outside and said, "Look up at the sky and count the stars—if indeed you can count them." Then he said to him, "So shall your offspring be."

LET'S LOOK AT ANOTHER EXAMPLE FROM THE BOOK OF ACTS

In Chapter 10 of the book of Acts, there was a devout and God-fearing man named Cornelius in a place called Caesarea, who received a vision from God. In this vision, he distinctly saw an angel of God, who came to him and told him to send men to Joppa to bring back a man named Simon who is called Peter.

In the meantime, Peter, based in Joppa, went up to his housetop to pray and becomes hungry. As he prays we are told that he falls into a trance and sees a vision of the heavens opening and a great sheet descending, filled with all kinds of animals, reptiles and birds of the air. A voice commands him to "rise, kill, and eat" the unclean animals. Peter is perplexed by the instruction, to which he replies "By no means, Lord; for I have never eaten anything that is common or unclean." The voice came to him again stating, "Do not call anything impure that God has made clean." (Acts 10:15 NIV)

In this vision, God was speaking about more than dietary concerns, He was actually speaking about people. God used a vision to teach Peter a new thing - that the Gentiles were not unclean and that the Gospel was for them too. While Peter was wondering about the meaning of the vision, the men sent by Cornelius arrived and the Spirit said to him, "Simon, three men are looking for you. So get up and go downstairs. Do not hesitate to go with them, for I have sent them." (Acts 10:19-23 NIV)

Peter went along with the men, arrived in Joppa and preached the Word. The Spirit of God fell, people were filled with the Holy Ghost, were baptised and so on.

ALL OF THIS TRANSPIRED BECAUSE GOD CHANGED PETER'S THINKING WITH A VISION.

"HE TOOK THE STARS IN THE SKY
and painted a new picture for him."

HE USED STARS BY NIGHT SAND BY DAY
GENESIS 15:3-5

What did God do to change Abraham's belief? He showed him an image... He took the stars in the sky and painted a picture for him.
At that time there was no canvas so He used the stars. He used the canvas of nature and told Abraham to look at it. That was Abraham's faith prop. We have a Dream Book as our canvas.

There may be a car you want. Take a picture of it and paste it on your dream-sheet and put it on your fridge. When you practically take this step, you are changing your thinking and raising your expectations.
God had Abraham looking at the stars at night and the grains of sand by day so that each time he would remember what God had promised.

For Abraham, this was a form of meditation. His dream was always before him night and day.
Having your dream constantly before your eyes is a way for you to transform your thinking to line up with God's Word and His will for your life.

05

DECLARING THE END RESULT. SPEAK THE WORD OVER YOUR DREAM!
Matthew 8:6-10, Rev 19:11-16, Ecc 9:4, Psalm 103:20-21, Psalm 35:27

ENGAGE THE POWERFUL CREATIVE FORCE OF THE TOUNGE
Proverbs 4:23, Habakkuk 2:2-3

STEP FIVE

YOU WERE MADE IN GOD'S IMAGE AND ABLE TO OPERATE IN HIS LIKENESS. (GENESIS 1:26) IN THE BEGINNING GOD CALLED FORTH LIGHT, ALTHOUGH THERE WAS DARKNESS! HE DIDN'T FOCUS ON THE DARKNESS, HE ONLY FOCUSED ON THE END RESULT—LIGHT. STOP LOOKING AT YOUR CURRENT CIRCUMSTANCES! CALL FORTH YOUR DREAM (CONFESSING THE 'MEDITATED SEED' DAILY UNTIL YOU WITNESS THE MANIFESTATION), AND DECLARE THE END RESULT FROM THE BEGINNING. (ISAIAH 46:10) AS CHILDREN OF THE MOST HIGH, WE HAVE A RIGHT TO CALL 'THINGS' THAT BE NOT AS THOUGH THEY ARE. (ROMANS 4:17)

START TODAY, COME INTO AGREEMENT WITH HIS UNFAILING WORD (HIS 'SEED') AND WATCH 'IT' WORK!

DECLARING THE END RESULT.

You are made in God's image and can operate in His likeness. You're made to operate just like your heavenly Father.

In the beginning, God called forth light, although there was darkness all around. He didn't focus on the darkness, He only focused on the end result: light! Stop looking at your current circumstances. Call forth your dream, confess the 'meditated seed' daily until manifestation, and declare the end result from the beginning (Isaiah 46:10). Call it the way you want it!

NOW TO DO THIS EFFECTIVELY, YOU NEED TO DISCOVER WHO YOU ARE IN THE REALM OF THE SPIRIT.

Proverbs 23:7 (KJV) says, "As a man thinketh in his heart so is he." You need to see yourself the way that God sees you — as a ruler — or you will never command the results of a ruler.

INSIDE YOU, THERE IS A KING DESPERATE FOR EXPRESSION.

A good example to illustrate this is found in Judges chapter 6 where Gideon is found hiding in the wine press.

The Midianites had completely stripped and devastated the land that he was living in, reducing God's people to abject poverty. The enemy hordes had destroyed the crops and plundered the countryside. God's people were found living in caves and dens while the enemy was living in their houses and driving their cars (a picture of the church). Then God finds Gideon and He transfers a 'new image' into his heart — the image of a ruler. After we see Gideon chasing the enemy, he is described by God as a " mighty warrior" (Judges 6:12). This time it's the enemy who is found hiding.

So, what happened here? Gideon discovered who he was. Christianity is not a religion, it is the manifestation of the life of God in mortal man. Being born again is not an adjustment of lifestyle. It is a mystery of re-creation. The Bible says "My people are destroyed for lack of knowledge," (Hosea 4:6 NKJV) and we would add, a lack of knowledge of who they are, where they are from, and what they are worth.

The Message Bible says it this way in Genesis 1:26-28:
God spoke: "Let us make human beings in our image, make them reflecting our nature, so they can be responsible for the fish in the sea, the birds in the air, the cattle, And, yes, Earth itself, and every animal that moves on the face of Earth." God created human beings; He created them godlike, reflecting God's nature. He created them male and female. God blessed them: "Prosper! Reproduce! Fill Earth! Take charge! Be responsible for fish in the sea and birds in the air, for every living thing that moves on the face of Earth."

Before the fall, Adam was an extraordinary supernatural individual. He operated at a miracle level and his mind functioned on a miracle wavelength. Adam was supernaturally in command and was tasked with naming all of God's creatures.

Now, there are over 1 million species of animals on the Earth. Not only did Adam have the extraordinary creativity to name them all, but he also had an incredible capacity to remember each one's name. There were 4 rivers in the garden but no bridge.

"MIGHTY WARRIOR!"

THERE IS A KING IN YOU

REMEMBER

Unfortunately, many Christians have been corrupted by their natural environment, and so have lost the understanding of their unique nature. It's like the story of the baby lion that grew up among the sheep. The cub adjusted so much to its new environment that it forgot that it was a lion. One day a lion visited the river where the sheep and cub were drinking water and roared. All the sheep ran away, including the ignorant cub. This continued for some time until one day, the cub saw its reflection in the river while drinking and realised it looked exactly like the lion! Subsequently, the next time the lion roared at them, the cub refused to run away but rather ran excitedly to the lion who in turn welcomed it into its midst. The cub crossed over from fear to boldness by understanding its true nature.

Another question to ask is how it was possible for Adam to move about so freely during the naming process. He must have had some mechanism for movement. We see a glimpse of this with Peter walking on the water in Matthew 14:29.

If all the fish were named by Adam and he wasn't a diver, he must have had the authority to operate inside water, to be able to name each fish.
He was operating in the garden of "no limits," and God said, "I want to bring you into that same kind of garden when you cannot be restricted" (Isaiah 51:3).

Sadly, Adam fell off that grace when he partook of the forbidden fruit.

God had warned Adam, "You must not eat from the tree of the knowledge of good and evil, for when you eat from it you will certainly die." (Genesis 2:17). When Adam disobeyed, a part of him died.

But what was it that died in Adam?

It was his spirit, the spirit that linked him to God —the engine room for supernatural feats and accomplishments.

When Jesus came and died for us on the cross, He won back what was lost in Adam. We can now operate on the same extraordinary platform that Adam once did. Being born again brings every Christian back up to an extraordinary status.

John 3:6 says, "Flesh gives birth to flesh, but the Spirit gives birth to spirit." So a man who is born again is a spirit being, not a human being. He was a human being when he had a dead spirit, but now that he is born again his spirit is regenerated, and he has become a spirit being. That's the mystery of re-creation.

Take a look at verse 8: "The wind blows wherever it pleases. You hear its sound, but you cannot tell where it comes from or where it is going. So it is with everyone born of the Spirit."

That's why the Bible says you determine the happenings, the wind blows where it pleases. This is the picture of dominion, it goes where it wants.

Whatever you don't want must go and whatever you desire must be delivered.

YOU HEAR ITS SOUND...

NOW, A SOUNDLESS CHRISTIAN IS A SIGNLESS CHRISTIAN.

Why? You're a king, and a king makes decrees and his orders are carried out. You must be heard for the supernatural to be released. Words are the switch that sets the supernatural in motion. Your mouth is a powerful weapon of authority ordained by God to keep you in perfect dominion. Jesus was saying everyone who is born of the Spirit is like the wind. You must make distinct sounds with your mouth concerning what you desire before you can see a sign in that direction.

Ecclesiastes 8:4 (NKJV) says, "Where the word of a king is, there is power; And who may say to him, "What are you doing?""

ANGELS ARE LISTENING TO YOUR COMMAND AS KING.

WHO YOU ARE...

Matthew 8:5-10
Now when Jesus had entered Capernaum, a centurion came to Him, pleading with Him, saying, "Lord, my servant is lying at home paralyzed, dreadfully tormented." And Jesus said to him, "I will come and heal him." The centurion answered and said, "Lord, I am not worthy that You should come under my roof. But only speak a word, and my servant will be healed. For I also am a man under authority, having soldiers under me. And I say to this one, 'Go,' and he goes; and to another, 'Come,' and he comes; and to my servant, 'Do this,' and he does it." When Jesus heard it, He marvelled, and said to those who followed, "Assuredly, I say to you, I have not found such great faith, not even in Israel!

PSALM 103:20
"PRAISE THE LORD, YOU HIS ANGELS, YOU MIGHTY ONES WHO DO HIS BIDDING, WHO OBEY HIS WORD."

The words you speak are so important because angels are listening to what you say. Many people think that God tells the angelic hosts what to do, but most of the time you give them their assignments. They stand beside you daily as ministering spirits listening to the words that come out of your mouth. They are working for you. 24 hours a day and 7 days a week! They require no overtime!

If your words are in line with God's Word, then the angels go to work immediately, causing the things you speak to come to pass. However, things that are contrary to God's Word will not get you an audience with angels. They won't operate on those words. Words spoken contrary to the Word of God will bind the angels. They are designed as ministering spirits to minister for you.

ANGELS MAKE THE WORD OF GOD EFFECTIVE.

Angels are the enforces of the Kingdom. They follow the Word of God, to make sure it produces results.

Revelations 19:11-16
I saw heaven standing open and there before me was a white horse, whose rider is called Faithful and True. With justice He judges and wages war. His eyes are like blazing fire, and on His head are many crowns. He has a name written on Him that no one knows but He Himself. He is dressed in a robe dipped in blood, and His name is the Word of God. The armies of heaven were following Him, riding on white horses and dressed in fine linen, white and clean. Coming out of His mouth is a sharp sword with which to strike down the nations. "He will rule them with an iron sceptre." He treads the winepress of the fury of the wrath of God Almighty. On His robe and on His thigh He has this name written:

"KING OF KINGS AND LORD OF LORDS"

In the above scripture, we see His name is called The Word of God, and that the armies of heaven followed the Word.

WHEN SOUND IS RELEASED ANGELS IMMEDIATELY GO TO WORK.

Some Christians have had really tough times on Earth. But, they didn't have to live that way. It was because they didn't realise the help that was available to them that they settled for less. They could have escaped lack, unpaid rent, empty grocery cupboards and cut electricity. They could have escaped sickness and premature death. They didn't escape these situations simply because they didn't use the ministering spirits (angels) sent forth to minister for them who are the heirs of salvation (Hebrews 1:14).

You have angels that are waiting for your words!

As written in Hebrews 2:1 "We must pay the most careful attention, therefore, to what we have heard, so that we do not drift away."

Your tongue is a powerful weapon given to you by God to overcome and triumph in life. When you know how to use it effectively it will change the direction of your life completely.

LET ME GIVE YOU A FEW EXAMPLES

OF HOW TO USE YOUR WORDS:

A few years back a lady came to visit my wife and me as she was battling to conceive a child. We gave her various scriptures to meditate on and confessions to make daily. The following morning I was in my secret place praising the Lord and the Holy Spirit prompted me to pray for this lady's womb. Within moments I held in my hands a womb. I was shocked, but I began to speak life into it and wrestled against any forces of darkness holding back this child as we are taught in Ephesians 6:12 (KJV) "We wrestle not against flesh and blood, but against principalities, against powers, against the rulers of the darkness of this world, against spiritual wickedness in high places."

I found myself making decrees over her womb in the spirit, forcing the spirit of barrenness to bow. A few weeks later, this same lady was giving God praise for the miracle that had taken place in her body.

She told us that her womb was twisted inside and that she had cysts on her ovaries. The doctors had tried various treatments but nothing had worked. Praise be to God the master physician who can fix the unfixable.

This lady had a dream, but it took spiritual knowledge and insight from God's Word to birth it and set her free.

In Ezekiel 37:1-14 there is a picture of this truth.

"The hand of the Lord was on me, and he brought me out by the Spirit of the Lord and set me in the middle of a valley; it was full of bones. 2 He led me back and forth among them, and I saw a great many bones on the floor of the valley, bones that were very dry."

In verse 2 we understand that the bones were very dry. Now, this lady's situation was very hopeless, humanly speaking. Dryness talks about lifelessness and helplessness. Remember, however, that the hand of the Lord carried Ezekiel in the Spirit of the Lord. That is the most effective state to be for prophecy or decrees to take place and have this effect. Being in the Spirit of the Lord is the right springboard for prophetic battles. Every time the Spirit of the Lord comes upon you, you have an initiation into the prophetic realm for doing battle.

Verse 4 says: "Then he said to me, "Prophesy to these bones and say to them, 'Dry bones, hear the word of the Lord!"

All we need is the Word of the Lord. That was the substance needed to create. He spoke God's Word to the hopeless situation. "Hear the Word of the Lord." When confronted with any situation, speak the Word of the Lord. Speaking the Word of God to negative situations amounts to prophesying to those situations, commanding life into very dry situations of life.

Verse 7 continues: "So I prophesied as I was commanded. And as I was prophesying, there was a noise, a rattling sound, and the bones came together, bone to bone." The bones were scattered and lifeless, but as Ezekiel prophesied, the bones came together, preceded by a great noise and shaking. Folks this is a mighty force. Many believers struggle through life, instead of triumphing. No force can resist the power of God's Word in your mouth declared from a faith-filled heart.

Verse 8 tells us that the tendons and flesh came upon the bones, as well as skin. "I looked, and tendons and flesh appeared on them and skin covered them, but there was no breath in them." They were still lifeless. Ezekiel was told to prophesy again in verse 9, but this time, to the winds to breathe upon the lifeless bodies, so they would live. "So I prophesied as he commanded me, and breath entered them; **they came to life and stood up on their feet—a vast army.**"

Maybe you are facing an impossible situation.

Maybe you are facing a huge mountain of unpaid bills.

The Bible says in Mark 11:23 that "Truly I tell you, if anyone says to this mountain, 'Go, throw yourself into the sea,' and does not doubt in their heart but believes that what they say will happen, it will be done for them."

If you are trusting God to settle debt, take copies of all your bills, and all the mail that represents your debt. Stick them up on your dream sheet. Start making these decrees on the authority of God's Word. Remember that angels are in place harkening unto the voice of the Lord.

You can pray something along these lines…

In Jesus Name, I call these debts paid in full. Debt I speak to you in Jesus Name, be paid and be gone! Dematerialise and cease to exist. I now declare on the authority of God's Word in Exodus 6:5 and Isaiah 10:27, that all my bills and any form of borrowing be paid in full, cancelled and dissolved.

Now, the easiest way to cancel your debt is with money! So, let me give you these confessions that I use to call in finance when needed.

HERE ARE TWO SECRETS!

Never allow the following words out of your mouth. Get around them in some kind of way. In the case where a salesperson is pushing you for an answer, never say "I can't afford it." Rather say, "I'll be back."

Never say, "I'm on a fixed income." By saying this, you have just stopped every unexpected cheque from coming into your hands.
Watch your words. They are either bringing increase or decrease to your life.

WEALTH FILES
DEUTERONOMY 8:18

UNLOCKING THE SECRETS OF HIDDEN WEALTH GOD HAS PLACED WITHIN YOU

OFFICIAL DOCUMENT

I DO NOT DEPEND ON PERSONS OR CONDITIONS FOR MY PROSPERITY AND SUPPLY… GOD IS THE SOURCE OF MY SUPPLY, SO I NOW PUT GOD FIRST FINANCIALLY. I TITHE MY WAY TO PROSPERITY.
THE VOLUNTARY FAITHFUL TITHING OF MY WHOLE INCOME NOW OPERATES THE LAW OF EVER INCREASING PROSPERITY. YES, I NOW TITHE MY WAY TO PEACE, HEALTH AND PLENTY. THERE IS NO NUMBERING OF THE AVENUES THROUGH WHICH SUPPLY CAN COME TO ME.

REMEMBER THE LORD YOUR GOD, FOR IT IS HE WHO GIVES YOU THE ABILITY TO PRODUCE WEALTH, AND SO CONFIRMS HIS COVENANT.

SCAN THIS QR CODE TO FIND MORE TRUTHS TO CONFESS OVER YOUR FINANCES.

WEALTH FILES

OFFICIAL DOCUMENT

● WHO HATH KNOWN THE MIND OF THE LORD, THAT HE MAY INSTRUCT HIM? 1 COR 2:16

WEALTH FILES
DEUTERONOMY 8:18
UNLOCKING THE SECRETS OF HIDDEN WEALTH GOD HAS PLACED WITHIN YOU

OFFICIAL DOCUMENT

I DO NOT DEPEND ON PERSONS OR CONDITIONS FOR MY PROSPERITY AND SUPPLY... GOD IS THE SOURCE OF MY SUPPLY, SO I NOW PUT GOD FIRST FINANCIALLY. I TITHE MY WAY TO PROSPERITY.
THE VOLUNTARY FAITHFUL TITHING OF MY WHOLE INCOME NOW OPERATES THE LAW OF EVER INCREASING PROSPERITY. YES, I NOW TITHE MY WAY TO PEACE, HEALTH AND PLENTY. THERE IS NO NUMBERING OF THE AVENUES THROUGH WHICH SUPPLY CAN COME TO ME.

○ REMEMBER THE LORD YOUR GOD, FOR IT IS HE WHO GIVES YOU THE ABILITY TO PRODUCE WEALTH, AND SO CONFIRMS HIS COVENANT.

WEALTH FILES
DEUTERONOMY 8:18
UNLOCKING THE SECRETS OF HIDDEN WEALTH GOD HAS PLACED WITHIN YOU

OFFICIAL DOCUMENT

WEALTH GET UP AND COME TO ME WHERE YOU ARE SUPPOSE TO BE, IN JESUS NAME!!!

○ REMEMBER THE LORD YOUR GOD, FOR IT IS HE WHO GIVES YOU THE ABILITY TO PRODUCE WEALTH, AND SO CONFIRMS HIS COVENANT.

WEALTH FILES
DEUTERONOMY 8:18
UNLOCKING THE SECRETS OF HIDDEN WEALTH GOD HAS PLACED WITHIN YOU

OFFICIAL DOCUMENT

BE THOU DISSOLVED IN THE NAME OF JESUS CHRIST.

EVERY FINANCIAL HASSLE YOU HAVE, EVERY FINANCIAL LACK YOU HAVE THAT IS CREEPING AROUND YOUR PLACE.

○ REMEMBER THE LORD YOUR GOD, FOR IT IS HE WHO GIVES YOU THE ABILITY TO PRODUCE WEALTH, AND SO CONFIRMS HIS COVENANT.

WEALTH FILES
DEUTERONOMY 8:18
UNLOCKING THE SECRETS OF HIDDEN WEALTH GOD HAS PLACED WITHIN YOU

OFFICIAL DOCUMENT

I WILL NEVER BE BROKE ANOTHER DAY IN MY LIFE. MONEY COMETH TO ME NOW, EASILY AND FREQUENTLY. I AM A MONEY MAGNET!

I HAVE A MILLIONAIRE STATUS ON THE INSIDE OF ME AND IT'S WORKING MIGHTILY! LET THE FINANCIAL MIRACLES BEGIN IN MY LIFE TODAY!
IN THE MIGHTY NAME OF JESUS.

○ REMEMBER THE LORD YOUR GOD, FOR IT IS HE WHO GIVES YOU THE ABILITY TO PRODUCE WEALTH, AND SO CONFIRMS HIS COVENANT.

WEALTH FILES
DEUTERONOMY 8:18
UNLOCKING THE SECRETS OF HIDDEN WEALTH GOD HAS PLACED WITHIN YOU

OFFICIAL DOCUMENT

I YIELD TO "THE BLESSING OF THE LORD." MY NEEDS, MY DESIRES AND MY DREAMS ARE BEING MET NOW. THE KINGDOM OF GOD IS ON THE INSIDE OF ME. I DRAW FROM "HIS" UNLIMITED KINGDOM

- POWER
- REVELATION
- ILLUMINATION
- INSPIRATION
- ANNOINTING
- INSIGHT
- ENLIGHTENMENT

○ REMEMBER THE LORD YOUR GOD, FOR IT IS HE WHO GIVES YOU THE ABILITY TO PRODUCE WEALTH, AND SO CONFIRMS HIS COVENANT.

WEALTH FILES
DEUTERONOMY 8:18
UNLOCKING THE SECRETS OF HIDDEN WEALTH GOD HAS PLACED WITHIN YOU

OFFICIAL DOCUMENT

ALL FINANCIAL DOORS ARE OPEN.
ALL FINANCIAL CHANNELS ARE FREE.
AN ENDLESS BOUNTY NOW COMES TO ME, IN JESUS NAME!
MY RESOURCE IS AS FAR REACHING AS THE UNIVERSE. I EXPECT MY SUPPLY THROUGH ALL AVENUES OF LIFE, FROM ALL POINTS OF THE WORLD, UNLIMITED SUPPLY IS CROWDING UPON ME NOW.

○ REMEMBER THE LORD YOUR GOD, FOR IT IS HE WHO GIVES YOU THE ABILITY TO PRODUCE WEALTH, AND SO CONFIRMS HIS COVENANT.

WEALTH FILES
DEUTERONOMY 8:18
UNLOCKING THE SECRETS OF HIDDEN WEALTH GOD HAS PLACED WITHIN YOU

OFFICIAL DOCUMENT

MY FINANCIAL INCOME CANNOT BE LIMITED NOW. THE RICH SUBSTANCE OF THE UNIVERSE NOW FREES ME FROM ALL FINANCIAL LIMITATIONS.
I LET GO OF WORN OUT THINGS, WORN OUT CONDITIONS AND WORN OUT RELATIONSHIPS, DEVINE ORDER IS NOW ESTABLISHED AND MAINTAINED IN ME AND IN MY WORLD. I AM RICH, WELL AND HAPPY AND EVERY PHASE OF MY LIFE IS IN DIVINE ORDER NOW.

○ REMEMBER THE LORD YOUR GOD, FOR IT IS HE WHO GIVES YOU THE ABILITY TO PRODUCE WEALTH, AND SO CONFIRMS HIS COVENANT.

WEALTH FILES
DEUTERONOMY 8:18
UNLOCKING THE SECRETS OF HIDDEN WEALTH GOD HAS PLACED WITHIN YOU

OFFICIAL DOCUMENT

I GET DEFINITE ABOUT PROSPERITY AND PROSPERITY GETS DEFINITE ABOUT ME. I HAVE PLENTY TO SHARE AND SPARE.

MY WORDS ARE CHARGED WITH PROSPERING POWER... X 5 TIMES "SAY IT LIKE YOU MEAN IT!
NOW! CAN YOU FEEL THE ATMOSPHERE CHANGING?
OUR WORDS ARE CREATIVE."

○ REMEMBER THE LORD YOUR GOD, FOR IT IS HE WHO GIVES YOU THE ABILITY TO PRODUCE WEALTH, AND SO CONFIRMS HIS COVENANT.

WEALTH FILES
DEUTERONOMY 8:18
UNLOCKING THE SECRETS OF HIDDEN WEALTH GOD HAS PLACED WITHIN YOU

OFFICIAL DOCUMENT

LARGE SUMS OF MONEY AND BIG HAPPENINGS, FINANCIAL SUPRISES AND RICH APPROPRIATE GIFTS NOW COME TO ME IN PERFECT WAYS FOR MY PERSONAL USE AND I USE THEM WISELY.

EVERYTHING AND EVERYBODY PROSPERS ME NOW AND I PROSPER EVERYTHING AND EVERYBODY NOW.

○ REMEMBER THE LORD YOUR GOD, FOR IT IS HE WHO GIVES YOU THE ABILITY TO PRODUCE WEALTH, AND SO CONFIRMS HIS COVENANT.

WEALTH FILES
DEUTERONOMY 8:18
UNLOCKING THE SECRETS OF HIDDEN WEALTH GOD HAS PLACED WITHIN YOU

OFFICIAL DOCUMENT

I DO NOT DEPEND ON PERSONS OR CONDITIONS FOR MY PROSPERITY AND SUPPLY. GOD IS THE SOURCE OF MY SUPPLY, SO I NOW PUT GOD FIRST FINANCIALLY. I TITHE MY WAY TO PROSPERITY. THE VOLUNTARY FAITHFUL TITHING OF MY WHOLE INCOME NOW OPERATES THE LAW OF EVER INCREASING PROSPERITY. I NOW TITHE MY WAY TO PEACE, HEALTH AND PLENTY. THERE IS NO NUMBERING OF THE AVENUES THROUGH WHICH SUPPLY CAN COME TO ME.

○ REMEMBER THE LORD YOUR GOD, FOR IT IS HE WHO GIVES YOU THE ABILITY TO PRODUCE WEALTH, AND SO CONFIRMS HIS COVENANT.

DAVID WAS A LITTLE BOY, WITH A BIG VOICE!

HE ALSO FACED AN IMPOSSIBLE SITUATION. HE KNEW THAT INSIDE OF HIM WAS A KING. DAVID USED 6 CONFESSIONS TO DEFEAT GOLIATH, AND TO END ISRAEL'S STRUGGLE IN A DAY!

DON'T WORRY ABOUT A THING, I'LL TAKE CARE OF THIS PHILISTINE
1 SAM 17:32

I'VE DONE THIS BOTH TO LION AND BEARS, AND I'LL DO IT TO THIS HEATHEN PHILISTINE TOO!
1 SAM 17:36

THE LORD WHO SAVED ME FROM THE CLAWS AND TEETH OF THE LION AND THE BEAR WILL SAVE ME FROM THIS PHILISTINE!
1 SAM 17:37

BUT I COME TO YOU IN THE NAME OF THE LORD OF THE ARMIES OF HEAVEN
1 SAM 17:45

TODAY THE LORD WILL CONQUER YOU AND I WILL KILL YOU AND CUT OFF YOUR HEAD!
1 SAM 17:46

THIS IS THE LORDS BATTLE AND HE WILL GIVE YOU TO US!
1 SAM 17:47

LET YOUR LIFE TESTIFY OF HIS GOODNESS AND THANK HIM FOR IT.

EXPERIENCE THE WONDERS OF GIVING GOD PRAISE...

STEP SIX

GIVE GOD ALL PRAISE FOR BRINGING YOUR DREAM TO PASS.
THE WORD SAYS IN REVELATIONS 12:11, "THEY OVERCAME BY THE BLOOD OF THE LAMB AND THE WORD OF THEIR TESTIMONY."
MATTHEW 5:14-16, 1 PETER 2:9

BY GIVING GOD PRAISE, YOU ARE INVITING THE ALMIGHTY TO STEP INTO YOUR SITUATION.
2 CHRONICLES 20-12, 15, 17-25; ACTS 16:25-26

LET YOUR LIFE TESTIFY OF HIS GOODNESS

Matthew 5:14-16 (NIV)
"You are the light of the world. A town built on a hill cannot be hidden. 15 Neither do people light a lamp and put it under a bowl. Instead they put it on its stand, and it gives light to everyone in the house. 16 In the same way, let your light shine before others, that they may see your good deeds and glorify your Father in heaven."

Don't hide what God is doing in your life. You are the light of the world. You are the ones that are to show the world a way forward. People are wanting to see evidence of your God, not just talk.

Faith without proof is fake! Faith is the substance of things hoped for, the evidence of things not seen. When it's void of evidence it's not faith, it's fake!

As a seed of Abraham, you are born to succeed. As a child of God you are created to add value to the world.

YOU ARE THE LIGHT OF THE WORLD. YOU ARE A PACE-SETTER, A PATHFINDER AND A TRAILBLAZER. AND, YOU SHOW THE WORLD THE WAY FORWARD.

You are ahead of this world. Light is ahead of darkness. So, if you are born again you are a role model to your generation. You are not just an ordinary person on the street. New birth makes you unique. Everyone should be looking up to you as a city set on a hill that cannot be hidden. Jesus came as a 'Star', the bright and morning star (Revelations 22:16). And, the Bible says, "As the Father has sent me, I am sending you." (Mark 20:21)

YOU ARE THE STARS THE WORLD IS WAITING FOR.

One of the vital forces for unlocking the supernatural is the force of testimonies. Testimonies establish the signs and wonders realm for the believer and that's where you belong.

Isaiah 8:18 "Here am I, and the children the Lord has given me. We are signs and symbols in Israel from the Lord Almighty, who dwells on Mount Zion."

It's important for you to understand that testimonies are as potent as the Word, because they are the proof of the Word and that the God who is behind them has not changed. We can use testimonies to see God do it again!

In 1 Samuel 17:33-37 we see how David overcame Goliath with his testimonies.

"Saul replied, "You are not able to go out against this Philistine and fight him; you are only a young man, and he has been a warrior from his youth." But David said to Saul, "Your servant has been keeping his father's sheep. When a lion or a bear came and carried off a sheep from the flock, I went after it, struck it and rescued the sheep from its mouth. When it turned on me, I seized it by its hair, struck it and killed it. Your servant has killed both the lion and the bear; this uncircumcised Philistine will be like one of them, because he has defied the armies of the living God. The Lord who rescued me from the paw of the lion and the paw of the bear will rescue me from the hand of this Philistine." Saul said to David, "Go, and the Lord be with you."

DAVID USED TESTIMONIES TO BRING DOWN GOLIATH.

What Goliaths are you facing today? When you testify what God has done, to someone else, it engages God to do it again! Testify continuously of God's goodness. Testimonies are prophetic seeds that must be sown so that others can reap a harvest and you can continue reaping the same over again (see Galatians 6:7 and John 12:24).

REVELATIONS 12:11 IS SO CLEAR: "THEY TRIUMPHED OVER HIM BY THE BLOOD OF THE LAMB AND BY THE WORD OF THEIR TESTIMONY; THEY DID NOT LOVE THEIR LIVES SO MUCH AS TO SHRINK FROM DEATH."

This was one of the first scriptures I learnt when I first came to Christ, and I worked this principle to overcome many negative circumstances. Our ministry seeks to give God praise with each product we produce.

We look forward to receiving and publishing testimonies of God's goodness and faithfulness because we've seen how testimonies are powerful tools for provoking the supernatural. The testimonies of your yesterday's victories are the weapons for today's victories. Your personal testimonies are treasures of inestimable value, to trade for the next triumph in your life.

You can use the testimonies of others for the victories you desire because God cannot deny himself (2 Timothy 2:13). God is no respecter of any person. You can be confident that what He has done for others He will do for you (Acts 10:34-35).

In the Book of Matthew, we learn about the woman who touched the hem of Jesus' garment and was made whole. From that time onwards, everybody was looking to touch the hem of His garment. Her testimony opened the gateway to many other victories.

THE TESTIMONIES OF YOUR TRIUMPH YESTERDAY ARE EFFECTIVE WEAPONS IN SECURING VICTORY IN TODAY'S BATTLE.

We need to be cognizant of the work God is doing in our lives and make sure we don't view it as ordinary or risk that He may cease to continue this work. Psalm 28:5 warns us of this, stating "Because they have no regard for the deeds of the Lord and what His hands have done, He will tear them down and never build them up again."

Psalm 78:9-12
"The men of Ephraim, though armed with bows, turned back on the day of battle; they did not keep God's covenant and refused to live by His law. They forgot what He had done, the wonders He had shown them. He did miracles in the sight of their ancestors in the land of Egypt, in the region of Zoan."

This Psalm refers to one of the 12 tribes of Israel that had forgotten God's works and the wonders that He had shown them.

Rather than heeding Psalm 119:2, (Blessed [are] they who keep His testimonies, [and who] seek Him with their whole heart), the men forgot the works of the Lord and turned back in battle. They were armed with bows and arrows to conquer the enemy but they forgot the Lord and were defeated.

So testimonies are our bows and arrows in dealing with the challenges of life. In Psalm 78:40-43 (NKJV) the Bible says, "How often they provoked Him in the wilderness, And grieved Him in the desert! Yes, again and again they tempted God, And limited the Holy One of Israel. They did not remember His power: The day when He redeemed them from the enemy, when He worked His signs in Egypt, And His wonders in the field of Zoan."

THEY DID NOT REMEMBER...

So they provoked God by not remembering His hand.

AMAZING TESTIMONIES IN YOUR LIFE WRITTEN OFF AS ORDINARY EVENTS

Psalm 78:56 (NKJV) "Yet they tested and provoked the Most High God, And did not keep His testimonies, But turned back and acted unfaithfully like their fathers; They were turned aside like a deceitful bow. For they provoked Him to anger with their high places, And moved Him to jealousy with their carved images."

When you say things like, "If I had known somebody, I would have got the job." Well, that's why you don't have it.

"The people who know their God shall be strong, and carry out great exploits." Daniel 11:32 (NKJV)

Let me also remind you; "Cursed is the one who trusts in man, who draws strength from mere flesh and whose heart turns away from the Lord. That person will be like a bush in the wastelands; they will not see prosperity when it comes. They will dwell in the parched places of the desert, in a salt land where no one lives." Jeremiah 17:5-6

The Israelites tempted and provoked the most high God and did not keep His testimonies.

Testimonies are the secret behind our strength in battle. *Included in your product pack is a testimony card.*

DON'T HIDE WHAT GOD IS DOING IN YOUR LIFE!

TESTIFY AND GIVE GOD PRAISE!

1 THESSALONIANS 5:18
"GIVE THANKS IN ALL CIRCUMSTANCES; FOR THIS IS GOD'S WILL FOR YOU IN CHRIST JESUS."

Take note that the Lord uses the word "in" not "for" in this verse. In every situation you find yourself, give thanks for this is the will of God. In every situation give thanks for that is how you gain command over everything.

You don't need to thank God for sickness, but in sickness, you can thank the Lord that He holds the key to recovery. You can thank the Lord that the price has been totally paid for your health. You can thank the Lord that He never lies. In everything give thanks for this is God's will for you in Christ Jesus.

"You need to persevere so that when you have done the will of God, you will receive what He has promised." Hebrews 10:36

Thank Him in advance for granting you the desires of your heart. I see God drawing amazing, enviable conclusions to your life.

On this side of heaven, we give thanks when things have been done, but in heaven where you belong, we give thanks for things to be done. That's the sacrifice of thanksgiving. Hebrews 13:15 puts it like this: "Through Jesus, therefore, let us continually offer to God a sacrifice of praise—the fruit of lips that openly profess His name."

On this side of heaven, we give thanks after things have happened. That's why many people are grounded today because they are waiting for things to happen. But nothing happens in the Kingdom until thanks have ascended to heaven. Jesus gave thanks in a situation of lack, and abundance answered. The Bible says Jesus knew what He would do when He was faced with feeding 5000 men excluding women and children. (John 6:6-13)

JESUS GAVE THANKS.

We can be thankful to the Lord for the 5 loaves and 2 fish and thank Him that He fed 3,000 000 people daily who were travelling from Egypt into the promised land. They were fed daily over a forty-year period. Where did the food come from? Heaven's storehouse. Not only did He feed them but they were fed a balanced diet of bread (manna) and meat (quail).

→ **SHARE YOUR STORY**

What are we telling you to do in an impossible situation?

THAT'S RIGHT, GIVE THANKS!

Thanksgiving confers the right of command upon your life over every situation around you. Even the spirit of death has to bow its head. Jesus gave thanks in John 11:41 and a dead Lazarus came forth.

A situation steeped in death will experience a dramatic turnaround with quality thanksgiving.

As you advance and start possessing the best of God, your promised land, remember in that land there are giants and they are stronger and mightier than you (see Deut. 7:1, Deut. 9:1).

As you journey forwards towards your dream, there may be battles you will encounter that seem mightier than your strength, far beyond your wisdom and as a result, you are unsure of what to do.

It's at these times that we need to hand the battle over to the One who can deal with it and the medium by which we do this is through praise.

GIVE GOD PRAISE AND HE WILL STEP INTO THE ARENA IN A WAY THAT NOBODY CAN DENY.

I remember sitting on our little boat with many other little boats all around us in the Durban Harbour. At times a huge ship would enter the harbour mouth and as it entered you would see these little boats scatter. Your praise has a very similar effect.

The Bible says, "May God arise, may His enemies be scattered; may His foes flee before Him" (Psalm 68:1). The King of Glory comes down to rescue you when your high praises ascend to heaven.

LET ME SHOW YOU AN EXAMPLE FROM THE BOOK OF ACTS:16:24-26.

"When he received these orders, he put them in the inner cell and fastened their feet in the stocks. About midnight **Paul and Silas were praying and singing hymns to God**, and the other prisoners were listening to them. Suddenly there was such a violent earthquake that the foundations of the prison were shaken. At once all the prison doors flew open, and everyone's chains came loose."

In verse 24, we see Paul and Silas thrust into prison and facing execution the following day. All the doors looked shut, the chains were locked, and the soldiers were standing by to see if there was going to be an attempted escape. But, in the midst of it, Paul and Silas began singing God's praises and the **ALMIGHTY STEPPED INTO THE BATTLE!**

As Paul and Silas's praises ascended to heaven, heaven came down for their rescue and suddenly there was a great earthquake that shook the foundations of the prison. **IMMEDIATELY**, all the doors were opened and everyone's bands were loosened. God is always responding to the high praises of His people and that includes you.

As you receive this revelation and start to praise Him, I would like you to prepare for sudden and immediate manifestations. Something supernatural is starting to happen in your life.

Immediately all the doors were opened. I see every door the enemy has shut concerning you opened in Jesus' name today. You have been kept in that prison house for long enough. Many have thought there will not be a way of escape but today amid your high praises, the King of Glory will show up.

When God shows up, your battle is over and all the prison doors will be opened. When He shows up your bands will be loosed. When He shows up the foundation of the prison shall be shaken and it will no longer have the capacity to hold you captive.

I SEE YOU WALKING OUT TODAY, AT LAST.

RUMBLE

SHAKE

BOOM!

PRAISE

WHO IS THIS KING OF GLORY? THE LORD STRONG AND MIGHTY, THE LORD MIGHTY IN BATTLE. LIFT UP YOUR HEADS, O YOU GATES; LIFT THEM UP, YOU ANCIENT DOORS, THAT THE KING OF GLORY MAY COME IN. WHO IS HE, THIS KING OF GLORY? THE LORD ALMIGHTY— HE IS THE KING OF GLORY. SELAH
PSALM 24:8-9

Keep praising Him and watch every gate be broken in pieces at His sight. Everything on this earth, including the mountains and the sea, trembles and skips like rams at His sight. Nothing can withstand His manifest presence. I see him stepping into your life and opening every door that has been shut for you.

Psalm 114:1-8
"When Israel came out of Egypt, Jacob from a people of foreign tongue, Judah became God's sanctuary, Israel his dominion. The sea looked and fled, the Jordan turned back; the mountains leaped like rams, the hills like lambs. Why was it, sea, that you fled? Why, Jordan, did you turn back? Why, mountains, did you leap like rams, you hills, like lambs? Tremble, earth, at the presence of the Lord, at the presence of the God of Jacob, who turned the rock into a pool, the hard rock into springs of water."

WHAT IS IN PRAISE AND WHAT MAKES IT SO EFFECTIVE IN BATTLE?

God is present everywhere BUT He does not manifest Himself everywhere. Matthew 18:20 tells us, "For where two or three gather in my name, there am I with them." He is always present BUT that is different from His manifest presence.

Let's look at this. In 2 Chronicles 20:12, 15, 17-25 tells us the story of Jehosaphat. In this story, we see that as all the people of Judah and Jerusalem fell down in worship before the Lord, God responded by sending ambushments against their enemies. Not one escaped. That's manifest presence.

As the people began to sing and to praise, God was aroused to manifest Himself and He set their enemies against one another and not one escaped (2 Chronicles 20: 22-24). God's manifest presence was provoked by their praise.

WHEN THE KING OF GLORY SHOWS UP ALL OPPOSITIONS BOW OUT.

When God shows up everlasting doors are opened and everlasting gates lift up their heads.

Psalm 24:7-10

"LIFT UP YOUR HEADS YOU GATES, YOU EVERLASTING DOORS, THAT THE KING OF GLORY MAY COME IN. WHO IS THIS KING OF GLORY? THE LORD MIGHTY IN BATTLE."

ENEMIES OF PRAISE

"Let the people praise thee, O God; let all the people praise thee. Then shall the earth yield her increase; and God, even our own God, shall bless us. God shall bless us; and all the ends of the earth shall fear Him. (Psalm 67:5-7)

The earth is not permitted to yield her increase without your praises. Your praises constitute a covenant trigger for your blessings. Many believers are addicted givers, yet many are not prospering. Why? **Because there is a missing key.**

The Bible says, "My people are destroyed for a lack of knowledge." (Hosea 4:6)

Here we must note that no murmurer is entitled to God's blessings. Every complainer complicates his case with God. Divine supplies will always respond to the praises of God's people. If you are not a praising believer you are not permitted to prosper. Giving is sowing the seed, but speaking positive words is watering the seed and high praises is reaping the harvest.

1 Corinthians 10:10
"Neither murmur ye, as some of them also murmured, and were destroyed of the destroyer."

The simple truth is that murmuring destroys. In the natural murmuring attracts sympathy but in the spiritual murmuring destroys. God has no patience with the murmurer.

They murmured and He destroyed them (Num 16:41,49) and He said "I am the Lord I change not."

Watch out, by the light breaking forth in your heart. Right now I see everything murmuring in you destroyed forever. God reacts in His anger to every murmurer because you do not regard the works of the Lord in your life or the operations of His hands.

According to Psalms 28:5 He says, "Because they regard not the works of the LORD, nor the operation of His hands, He shall destroy them, and not build them up".

When one man says something like, "nothing has happened to me this year," while the same man wakes up every morning strong and healthy, his wife and children the same.

God isn't there anymore, because they regard not the works of the Lord, nor the operation of His hands. He shall destroy them, and not build them up. The enemy's tactic is to push you to murmur, and in doing so you destroy yourself because the enemy knows that God has no patience with murmurers.

Many people are left stranded because they are complainers.

PRAISE IS THE GATEWAY TO EXPERIENCING THE MANIFEST PRESENCE OF GOD.

Praise is not entertainment.

When the ministers stood in the temple, the glory of God came down because they were not entertaining, they were provoking the manifest presence of God.

Look at David, it's no wonder he never lost a battle.

This was David's Prayer at the opening of the temple. Look at how he praised God.

1 CHRONICLES 29:9
THE PEOPLE REJOICED AT THE WILLING RESPONSE OF THEIR LEADERS, FOR THEY HAD GIVEN FREELY AND WHOLEHEARTEDLY TO THE LORD. DAVID THE KING ALSO REJOICED GREATLY."

DAVID'S PRAYER

David praised the Lord in the presence of the whole assembly, saying, "Praise be to you, Lord, the God of our father Israel, from everlasting to everlasting. Yours, Lord, is the greatness and the power and the glory and the majesty and the splendour, for everything in heaven and earth is yours. Yours, Lord, is the kingdom; you are exalted as head over all. Wealth and honour come from you; you are the ruler of all things. In your hands are strength and power to exalt and give strength to all. Now, our God, we give you thanks, and praise your glorious name. "But who am I, and who are my people, that we should be able to give as generously as this? Everything comes from you, and we have given you only what comes from your hand.

1 CHRONICLES 29:10-14,16

YOU WILL NEVER LEAVE WHERE YOU ARE UNTIL YOU **SEE A PICTURE** OF WHERE YOU WANT TO BE

MY DREAM

THIS IS WHERE YOU WRITE DOWN YOUR DREAM, EITHER BIG OR SMALL
EPHESIANS 3:20

MY DREAM IS TO BUILD OUR OWN FAMILY HOME

DATE: 22/04/09

FOUNDATION SEED: HOUSES FILLED WITH ALL KINDS OF GOOD THINGS YOU DID NOT PROVIDE, WELLS YOU DID NOT DIG, AND VINEYARDS & OLIVE GROVES YOU DID NOT PLANT. DEUTERONOMY 6:10-12

THE DETAILS: OLD FRENCH STYLE. DEEP VERANDAH WITH FRONT STAIR WAY TO FRONT DOOR. BAY WINDOWS, WHITE TIN ROOF, HIGH CEILINGS, WOODEN FLOORS THROUGHOUT. NATURAL STONE FLOORING IN BATHROOMS, VERANDAH + COURTYARDS. CRESTWOOD KITCHEN WITH SOLID ROSEWOOD TOPS, A FRENCH TECHNIQUED CUPBOARDS. ALL 4 BEDROOMS ENSUITE. MUST HAVE A SECRET PLACE OR STUDY + GYM. SMEG APPLIANCES IN KITCHEN. ENTERTAINMENT AREA WITH POOL & BRAAI AREA. FLAT GARDEN. PROPERTY TO BE SITUATED IN KLOOF GOLF COURSE AREA. FIREPLACE IN LOUNGE, AND UNDER FLOOR HEATING PLUS CENTRAL AIR-CONDITIONING.

 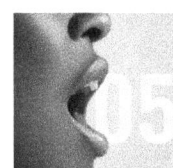

SEE STEP 4 & 5 ON DREAMSHEET

What is your greatest desire? What would you like to accomplish more than anything else in your life? What would you attempt to do if you knew it was impossible to fail?
Ephesians 3:20

TELL YOUR STORY

DATE ANSWERED: 22/04/09
DETAILS: THANK YOU LORD FOR GIVING US ALL THE DESIRES OF OUR HEART. THANK YOU FOR GIVING US OUR LAND IN THE AREA WE WANTED, AS WELL AS PROVIDING EVERYTHING TO BRING TO PASS OUR DREAM HOME.

Testify! Give God praise for bringing to pass your dream. The Word says in Revelations 12:11 "THEY OVERCAME BY THE BLOOD OF THE LAMB AND THE WORD OF THEIR TESTIMONY".

WE WOULD LOVED TO HEAR YOU STORY

EXAMPLE PAGE

THE DETAILS CONTINUED. DONT BE SHY...

BUILDING MATERIALS:
TILES
BATHROOM 1
WALL - TRAVENTINE CREME R260/M2
FLOOR - TRAVENTINE R260/M2
SHOWER - TRAVENTINE TUMBLES R400/M2

BATHROOM 2
WALL - TRAVENTINE CREME R260/M2
FLOOR - TRAVELINE R260/M2
SHOWER - TRAVENTINE TUMBLES R400/M2
TONGUE AND GROOVE
GLASS SHOWER - SHOWERLOINE (SPECAIL ORDER) +- R10 000,00
SHOWER HEADS & MIXES R5000.00
BATH (WITH JETS) BOUTIQUE BATHS R15 000.00
BATHROOM CUPBOARD (CRESTWOOD) R4500.00
GRANITE TOP R1500
SKYLOINE R2500
CEILOINGS R2000
DOWNLIGHTS (SPAZIO) AND ELECTRICAL R1500
BASIN & LOO R2500
MATERIALS & PLUMBER R5000

GUEST SUITE
WALL - TRAVENTINE CREME R260/M2
FLOOR - TRAVENTINE R260/M2
BLINDS - WHITE PATTERN R450

PAINTING
WALLS - BALLITO SAND R4000.00
CEILING WHITE +- R1500.00
PAINTING CONTRACT +- R3000

EXAMPLE PAGE

MY PINBOARD

PIN YOUR IMAGES
Start building your dream. Use a pinboard, fridge, mirror, computer screen. Any visible surface!

PREFER DIGITAL?
Scan QR code to access our pinterest page for inspiration.

Dream House Board

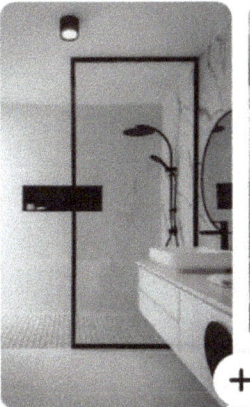

EXAMPLE PAGE

MY DREAM

THIS IS WHERE YOU WRITE DOWN YOUR DREAM, EITHER BIG OR SMALL
EPHESIANS 3:20

What is your greatest desire? What would you like to accomplish more than anything else in your life? What would you attempt to do if you knew it was impossible to fail?
Ephesians 3:20

_____

DATE: _____

TELL YOUR STORY

DATE ANSWERED: _____
DETAILS: _____

FOUNDATION SEED: _____
_____
_____

_____
_____
_____
_____
_____
_____
_____
_____
_____
_____
_____
_____
_____
_____
_____
_____
_____
_____

THE DETAILS: _____
_____
_____
_____
_____
_____
_____
_____
_____

SEE STEP 4 & 5 ON DREAMSHEET

Testify! Give God praise for bringing to pass your dream. The Word says in Revelations 12:11 " THEY OVERCAME BY THE BLOOD OF THE LAMB AND THE WORD OF THEIR TESTIMONY".

WE WOULD LOVED TO HEAR YOU STORY (QR CODE)

THE DETAILS CONTINUED. DONT BE SHY...

> THE DAY YOU MAKE A DECISION ABOUT YOUR LIFE, IS THE DAY YOUR WORLD WILL CHANGE.

MY DREAM

THIS IS WHERE YOU WRITE DOWN YOUR DREAM, EITHER BIG OR SMALL
EPHESIANS 3:20

_____

DATE: _____

FOUNDATION SEED: _____
_____
_____

THE DETAILS: _____
_____
_____
_____
_____
_____
_____
_____
_____

SEE STEP 4 & 5 ON DREAMSHEET

What is your greatest desire? What would you like to accomplish more than anything else in your life? What would you attempt to do if you knew it was impossible to fail?
Ephesians 3:20

TELL YOUR STORY

DATE ANSWERED: _____
DETAILS: _____
_____
_____
_____
_____
_____
_____
_____
_____
_____
_____
_____
_____
_____
_____
_____
_____
_____

Testify! Give God praise for bringing to pass your dream. The Word says in Revelations 12:11 " THEY OVERCAME BY THE BLOOD OF THE LAMB AND THE WORD OF THEIR TESTIMONY".

WE WOULD LOVED TO HEAR YOU STORY (QR CODE)

THE DETAILS CONTINUED. DONT BE SHY...

WRITING DOWN YOUR GOALS MAKES YOU MORE DECISIVE.

MY DREAM

THIS IS WHERE YOU WRITE DOWN YOUR DREAM, EITHER BIG OR SMALL
EPHESIANS 3:20

What is your greatest desire? What would you like to accomplish more than anything else in your life? What would you attempt to do if you knew it was impossible to fail?
Ephesians 3:20

_____

DATE: _____

FOUNDATION SEED: _____
_____
_____
_____

THE DETAILS: _____
_____
_____
_____
_____
_____
_____
_____
_____
_____

SEE STEP 4 & 5 ON DREAMSHEET

TELL YOUR STORY

DATE ANSWERED: _____
DETAILS: _____
_____
_____
_____
_____
_____
_____
_____
_____
_____
_____
_____
_____
_____
_____
_____
_____
_____

Testify! Give God praise for bringing to pass your dream. The Word says in Revelations 12:11 "THEY OVERCAME BY THE BLOOD OF THE LAMB AND THE WORD OF THEIR TESTIMONY".

WE WOULD LOVED TO HEAR YOU STORY (QR CODE)

THE DETAILS CONTINUED. DONT BE SHY...

RESPECT IS NEEDED FOR
EXCITEMENT
EXCITEMENT IS NEEDED FOR
ENERGY
ENERGY IS NEEDED FOR
COMPLETION OF YOUR
GOALS

MY DREAM

THIS IS WHERE YOU WRITE DOWN YOUR DREAM, EITHER BIG OR SMALL
EPHESIANS 3:20

_____

DATE: _____

FOUNDATION SEED: _____
_____
_____

THE DETAILS: _____
_____
_____
_____
_____
_____
_____
_____

SEE STEP 4 & 5 ON DREAMSHEET

What is your greatest desire? What would you like to accomplish more than anything else in your life? What would you attempt to do if you knew it was impossible to fail?
Ephesians 3:20

TELL YOUR STORY

DATE ANSWERED: _____
DETAILS: _____
_____
_____
_____
_____
_____
_____
_____
_____
_____
_____
_____
_____
_____
_____
_____

Testify! Give God praise for bringing to pass your dream. The Word says in Revelations 12:11 " THEY OVERCAME BY THE BLOOD OF THE LAMB AND THE WORD OF THEIR TESTIMONY".

WE WOULD LOVED TO HEAR YOU STORY (QR CODE)

THE DETAILS CONTINUED. DONT BE SHY...

WHATEVER CREATES JOY AND EXCITMENT WITHIN YOU, IS PROBABLY AN INDICATION OF WHAT GOD WANTS YOU TO PERSUE.

MY DREAM

THIS IS WHERE YOU WRITE DOWN YOUR DREAM, EITHER BIG OR SMALL
EPHESIANS 3:20

01 What is your greatest desire? What would you like to accomplish more than anything else in your life? What would you attempt to do if you knew it was impossible to fail?
Ephesians 3:20

_____

DATE: _____

FOUNDATION SEED: _____
_____
_____

THE DETAILS: _____
_____
_____
_____
_____
_____
_____
_____
_____
_____

SEE STEP 4 & 5 ON DREAMSHEET

TELL YOUR STORY

DATE ANSWERED: _____
DETAILS: _____
_____
_____
_____
_____
_____
_____
_____
_____
_____
_____
_____
_____
_____
_____
_____

06 Testify! Give God praise for bringing to pass your dream. The Word says in Revelations 12:11 "THEY OVERCAME BY THE BLOOD OF THE LAMB AND THE WORD OF THEIR TESTIMONY".

WE WOULD LOVED TO HEAR YOU STORY (QR CODE)

THE DETAILS CONTINUED. DONT BE SHY...

> **RESPECT YOUR DREAMS AND GOALS**
> WHAT YOU RESPECT
> **YOU WILL ATTRACT**

MY DREAM

THIS IS WHERE YOU WRITE DOWN YOUR DREAM, EITHER BIG OR SMALL

EPHESIANS 3:20

_____

DATE: _____

FOUNDATION SEED: _____
_____
_____

THE DETAILS: _____
_____
_____
_____
_____
_____
_____
_____
_____
_____

SEE STEP 4 & 5 ON DREAMSHEET

What is your greatest desire? What would you like to accomplish more than anything else in your life? What would you attempt to do if you knew it was impossible to fail?
Ephesians 3:20

TELL YOUR STORY

DATE ANSWERED: _____
DETAILS: _____
_____
_____
_____
_____
_____
_____
_____
_____
_____
_____
_____
_____
_____
_____
_____
_____
_____
_____

Testify! Give God praise for bringing to pass your dream. The Word says in Revelations 12:11 " THEY OVERCAME BY THE BLOOD OF THE LAMB AND THE WORD OF THEIR TESTIMONY".

WE WOULD LOVED TO HEAR YOU STORY (QR CODE)

THE DETAILS CONTINUED. DONT BE SHY...

WHAT YOU MAKE HAPPEN FOR OTHERS, GOD WILL MAKE HAPPEN FOR YOU.

MY DREAM

THIS IS WHERE YOU WRITE DOWN YOUR DREAM, EITHER BIG OR SMALL
EPHESIANS 3:20

_____

DATE: _____

FOUNDATION SEED: _____
_____
_____

THE DETAILS: _____
_____
_____
_____
_____
_____
_____
_____
_____

SEE STEP 4 & 5 ON DREAMSHEET

What is your greatest desire? What would you like to accomplish more than anything else in your life? What would you attempt to do if you knew it was impossible to fail?
Ephesians 3:20

TELL YOUR STORY

DATE ANSWERED: _____
DETAILS: _____
_____
_____
_____
_____
_____
_____
_____
_____
_____
_____
_____
_____
_____
_____
_____
_____
_____

Testify! Give God praise for bringing to pass your dream. The Word says in Revelations 12:11 " THEY OVERCAME BY THE BLOOD OF THE LAMB AND THE WORD OF THEIR TESTIMONY".

WE WOULD LOVED TO HEAR YOU STORY (QR CODE)

THE DETAILS CONTINUED. DONT BE SHY...

ONE HOUR WITH THE HOLY SPIRIT WILL REVEAL TO YOU ANY FLAWS IN YOUR MOST CAREFULLY LAID PLANS.

MY DREAM

THIS IS WHERE YOU WRITE DOWN YOUR DREAM, EITHER BIG OR SMALL
EPHESIANS 3:20

_____

DATE: _____

FOUNDATION SEED: _____
_____
_____

THE DETAILS: _____
_____
_____
_____
_____
_____
_____
_____

SEE STEP 4 & 5 ON DREAMSHEET

What is your greatest desire? What would you like to accomplish more than anything else in your life? What would you attempt to do if you knew it was impossible to fail?
Ephesians 3:20

TELL YOUR STORY

DATE ANSWERED: _____
DETAILS: _____
_____
_____
_____
_____
_____
_____
_____
_____
_____
_____
_____
_____
_____
_____
_____

Testify! Give God praise for bringing to pass your dream. The Word says in Revelations 12:11 " THEY OVERCAME BY THE BLOOD OF THE LAMB AND THE WORD OF THEIR TESTIMONY".

WE WOULD LOVED TO HEAR YOU STORY (QR CODE)

THE DETAILS CONTINUED. DONT BE SHY...

> WHEN YOU FOCUS ON **YOUR DREAM** YOU WILL **ELIMINATE CONFUSION**

MY DREAM

THIS IS WHERE YOU WRITE DOWN YOUR DREAM, EITHER BIG OR SMALL
EPHESIANS 3:20

What is your greatest desire? What would you like to accomplish more than anything else in your life? What would you attempt to do if you knew it was impossible to fail?
Ephesians 3:20

_____

DATE: _____

FOUNDATION SEED: _____
_____
_____
_____

THE DETAILS: _____
_____
_____
_____
_____
_____
_____
_____
_____
_____

SEE STEP 4 & 5 ON DREAMSHEET

TELL YOUR STORY

DATE ANSWERED: _____
DETAILS: _____
_____
_____
_____
_____
_____
_____
_____
_____
_____
_____
_____
_____
_____
_____
_____
_____

Testify! Give God praise for bringing to pass your dream. The Word says in Revelations 12:11 "THEY OVERCAME BY THE BLOOD OF THE LAMB AND THE WORD OF THEIR TESTIMONY".

WE WOULD LOVED TO HEAR YOU STORY (QR CODE)

THE DETAILS CONTINUED. DONT BE SHY...

PLANNERS CAN PREDICT THEIR SUCCESS.

MY DREAM

THIS IS WHERE YOU WRITE DOWN YOUR DREAM, EITHER BIG OR SMALL
EPHESIANS 3:20

What is your greatest desire? What would you like to accomplish more than anything else in your life? What would you attempt to do if you knew it was impossible to fail?
Ephesians 3:20

DATE: _____

FOUNDATION SEED: _____
_____
_____
_____

TELL YOUR STORY

DATE ANSWERED: _____
DETAILS: _____
_____
_____
_____
_____
_____
_____
_____
_____
_____
_____
_____
_____
_____
_____
_____
_____
_____

THE DETAILS: _____
_____
_____
_____
_____
_____
_____
_____
_____
_____
_____

SEE STEP 4 & 5 ON DREAMSHEET

Testify! Give God praise for bringing to pass your dream. The Word says in Revelations 12:11 " THEY OVERCAME BY THE BLOOD OF THE LAMB AND THE WORD OF THEIR TESTIMONY".

WE WOULD LOVED TO HEAR YOU STORY (QR CODE)

THE DETAILS CONTINUED. DONT BE SHY...

> **GOD REWARDS REACHERS! YOU WILL NEVER POSSESS WHAT YOU ARE UNWILLING TO REACH FOR**

MY DREAM

THIS IS WHERE YOU WRITE DOWN YOUR DREAM, EITHER BIG OR SMALL
EPHESIANS 3:20

What is your greatest desire? What would you like to accomplish more than anything else in your life? What would you attempt to do if you knew it was impossible to fail?
Ephesians 3:20

_____

DATE: _____

FOUNDATION SEED: _____
_____
_____
_____

THE DETAILS: _____
_____
_____
_____
_____
_____
_____
_____

SEE STEP 4 & 5 ON DREAMSHEET

TELL YOUR STORY

DATE ANSWERED: _____
DETAILS: _____
_____
_____
_____
_____
_____
_____
_____
_____
_____
_____
_____
_____
_____
_____
_____
_____
_____

Testify! Give God praise for bringing to pass your dream. The Word says in Revelations 12:11 " THEY OVERCAME BY THE BLOOD OF THE LAMB AND THE WORD OF THEIR TESTIMONY".

WE WOULD LOVED TO HEAR YOU STORY (QR CODE)

THE DETAILS CONTINUED. DONT BE SHY...

> **FOCUS ON ON TASKS THAT YOU FEEL ARE WORTHY OF YOUR TOTAL ATTENTION AND TIME.**

MY DREAM

THIS IS WHERE YOU WRITE DOWN YOUR DREAM, EITHER BIG OR SMALL
EPHESIANS 3:20

What is your greatest desire? What would you like to accomplish more than anything else in your life? What would you attempt to do if you knew it was impossible to fail?
Ephesians 3:20

_____

DATE: _____

FOUNDATION SEED: _____
_____
_____

THE DETAILS: _____
_____
_____
_____
_____
_____
_____
_____
_____

SEE STEP 4 & 5 ON DREAMSHEET

TELL YOUR STORY

DATE ANSWERED: _____
DETAILS: _____
_____
_____
_____
_____
_____
_____
_____
_____
_____
_____
_____
_____
_____
_____
_____
_____
_____
_____

Testify! Give God praise for bringing to pass your dream. The Word says in Revelations 12:11 " THEY OVERCAME BY THE BLOOD OF THE LAMB AND THE WORD OF THEIR TESTIMONY".

WE WOULD LOVED TO HEAR YOU STORY (QR CODE)

THE DETAILS CONTINUED. DONT BE SHY...

REFUSE TO QUIT

THE SECRET OF CHAMPIONS IS THEIR REFUSAL TO QUIT TRYING. REMEMBER EVEN THE WORLDS TALLEST BUILDINGS ARE BUILT **ONE BRICK AT A TIME.**

www.ingramcontent.com/pod-product-compliance
Lightning Source LLC
Chambersburg PA
CBHW041239240426
43661CB00071B/2922